One Religion Too Many

One Religion Too Many

The Religiously Comparative Reflections of a Comparatively Religious Hindu

Arvind Sharma

SUNY
PRESS

Published by State University of New York Press, Albany

Printed in the United States of America

For information, contact State University of New York Press, Albany, NY
www.sunypress.edu

Production by Kelli W. LeRoux
Marketing by Anne M. Valentine

Library of Congress Cataloging-in-Publication Data

Sharma, Arvind.
One religion too many : the religiously comparative reflections of a comparatively religious Hindu / Arvind Sharma.
p. cm.
Includes bibliographical references.
ISBN 978-1-4384-3247-2 (hardcover : alk. paper)
ISBN 978-1-4384-3248-9 (pbk. : alk. paper)
1. Sharma, Arvind. 2. Hindus—Biography. 3. Hinduism—Relations. 4. Religions. I. Title.

BL1175.S4235A35 2010
294.5092—dc22 2010004839

10 9 8 7 6 5 4 3 2 1

Contents

PART III

Preface

I try to tell the story of my engagement with religion within the covers of this book, but to a certain extent, it is an undercover operation. One has to spy on oneself to talk about one's religion as well as that of others. There are obvious pitfalls in doing so. One could display understanding without information in talking about one's religion—and information without understanding in talking about that of another. Only the reader can tell whether and to what degree these pitfalls have been avoided. It has been said that little of what a person tells about himself is accurate. But is not what one tells about oneself, in one sense, always true?

I did ask myself the following question occasionally as I was writing this memoir: Would I have written this memoir the way I have written it now, five years ago? And would I write it the way I have written it now, five years from now? Does not memory knit the fabric of recollection differently at different times? But then memory can knit and unknit forever like Penelope—waiting for the truth to arrive.

Acknowledgement

I would like to thank Motilal Banarsidass for permission to cite pages 22–25 and 161–67 of the book Storytellers, *Saints and Scoundrels: Folk Narratives in Hindu Religious Teaching* by Kirin Narayan.

Introduction

As one goes through life, one first acquires implicit knowledge of the diversity of one's own tradition and then the explicit knowledge of the diversity represented by the world's great religions. This book is an account of the changing attitudes of a student of religion toward religion in its internal and external variety. But it is also much more. It hints at the possibility that in the end one might emerge with the tacit knowledge of being the legatee of not just one's tradition (in this case Hinduism), however tolerant, or the various religious traditions of humanity, however diverse—but of the entire religious heritage of humanity as a whole.

The experience could be compared to that of geographical discovery, when what one thought was one's separate country turns out to be part of a continent; and then, what one thought were different continents, turn out to be part of a single globe. It is a long journey from *one* to *one*, from one country to one globe—and although one arrives back at the starting point, in a manner so dear to the mystical path—it is no longer the same starting place. What seemed like a circle turns out to be a spiral. For the spiral does not circle; neither does it encircle but ever opens out to new evolutions without denying earlier convolutions.

Each of these phases also seems to possess its own epistemology. I learnt about Hinduism experientially and unconsciously, but my knowledge of humanity's other religious traditions was acquired more intellectually, even academically.

The tendency to view the world's religions in their totality as the religion of humanity was acquired emotively. I hesitate to use the word *emotionally* because of the connotations of the word. It almost always seems to carry a hint of emotional turbulence. The acquisition of the sense of being the inheritor of all of humanity's religions traditions (and not just one) did not involve any such turbulence, rather the opposite. To borrow Wordsworth's famous definition of poetry, it was more akin to emotions recollected in tranquility.

I might go further and say that the realization was subjective, in the sense that I felt my religious psyche was a theater, and all the religious traditions were equally present in the theater. It was also subjective in the sense that I felt myself to be the subject of all the religious traditions on the one hand and subject to none on the other. There was certain blindness in relation to my religious tradition in a way, but it was the opposite of the blindness which comes from religious fanaticism—which consists in being blinded by the intensity of the luminosity of one's tradition by standing too close to it, instead of witnessing the entire world transfigured in its light. My knowledge of my own tradition was personal, and that of the various religions of the world empathetic, but the realization of all of these as belonging to one, rather than as constituting one's belongings, was subjective.

The attempt at the philosophical location of this experience carries a certain fascination with it. Hegel speaks in terms of abstract universality, abstract particularity, and concrete universality. He speaks in these terms because they embody distinct moments. Thus, abstract universality involves undifferentiated identity, while abstract particularity is able to relate to subcategories within the abstract universality—as one might distinguish men and women within the abstract universality of human beings. Similarly, while abstract universality may speak of the religious person, abstract particularity may speak of a Hindu or a Christian. Then, concrete universality indicates the coming together of these two moments. While it is tempting to place this grid on the configuration of my own religious experience, it might be truer to say in my case that, being a Hindu in India, was a moment of abstract universality (yes, abstract universality because of the way Hinduism tends to view all religions homogeneously), and the case of my being a comparative religionist in the West was a moment of abstract particularity. But the parallel ends here. The third stage of universality was not one of concrete universality in the sense that the moment of unity of all religions and the moment of diversity of all religions were equally present in it. It involved rather the loss of both forms of abstraction and the concrete realization of a religious tradition of humanity. Perhaps Adi Shankara provides a better parallel here, when he criticizes the *bhedābheda* doctrine that Brahman involves both identity and difference—an idea which at least bears a superficial resemblance to that of concrete universality. If sameness or unity is an abstraction from one point of view—and diversity or difference is also from another—then the two taken together do not cancel out the abstraction. Their combination could also be an abstraction.

Perhaps, the point is best made by modifying the metaphor at this point and by saying that, whereas in the first two stages one feels one is dealing with maps, one now has the feeling of having put one's foot on the territory in the third stage. Starting as a cartographer one becomes a traveler. And once you become a traveler, the significance of the lines on the map changes, even though the lines may not change. One is concerned now with relevance rather than the possibility of syncretism.

The different epistemologies involved also influence the style of presentation in the three parts of my book. The presentation in the first part is in the accordance with the places where I grew up—some of which may seem exotic, others familiar. The presentation in the second part is in line not with places but religions; it deals not so much with physical as cerebral sojourns. My presentation in the third part is in the form of events.

A Sufi account provides a good clue for bringing these remarks to a close, specially if one chooses to look upon one's religious tradition as something one possesses rather than as something one is possessed by. The Sufis say that one's attitude toward one's possessions passes through three stages as one progresses along the mystical path. As one starts out on the path, one says or believes, "Yours is yours and mine is mine." As one progresses on it further, one begins to believe and says, "Yours is yours and mine is also yours." And finally, a stage is reached when one says, "There is neither mine nor thine." My account stays within the basic boundaries of this process but allows us to ring a few minor changes. I started out by saying, "Mine is mine (and yours is also in it)," the Hindu phase. Then, I reached a stage when I could say, "Mine is mine and yours is mine too," the comparative phase. And finally, I come to the present phase: "All of it is ours."

PART I

Banaras

A Hindu is not born; a Hindu is reborn. It might seem preposterous to begin a narrative of my religious life, which began in India, with a reference to Johnny Carson, the king of American TV. In a globalized world, however, anything is possible. As I watched the show one night, Carson narrated how on his show someone had actually claimed that he remembered being born. That was when I realized once again that I was a Hindu because I wondered: wouldn't it be neat if I remembered not only being *born* but being *reborn*. We do not know whether this is a case of culture imposing itself on nature, as sceptical students of religion might claim—or a case of culture merely recognizing a fact of nature, which has eluded the grasp of other cultures, as the rebirthing Hindu might claim. Nevertheless, right here I possessed a key ingredient of not just the Hindu but the Indic world view. An amazing idea—coming to think of it—that we have been here before, that this life is merely a link in an endless chain stretching so far back into the past that the Buddha had to exclaim, "As far as I can see, O Monks, I see no beginning."[1] And this coming from one who had been capable of looking further into the rearview mirror of life than anyone else. I might say that belief in rebirth is as self-evident to many in India as belief in God is to those who believe in one. It is too self-evident to be in need of proof. It is not a thesis to be proved but a fact to be elaborated.

The Buddha himself once did so famously when he was sitting in a gathering of monks and nuns and suddenly one of the nuns burst into tears. If this happened to someone in an audience as I was lecturing, I don't know what I would do, but the Buddha smiled. And when the brethren asked him why he smiled, he told this story:

The Six-tusked Elephant

Once upon a time the Buddha-elect was born as the son of the elephant chief of a herd of eight thousand royal elephants, who lived near to a great lake in the Himalayas. In the middle of this lake was clear water, and round this grew sheets of white and coloured water-lilies, and fields of rice and gourds and sugar-cane and plantains; it was surrounded by a bamboo grove and a ring of great mountains. In the north-east corner of the lake grew a huge banyan-tree, and on the west side there was an enormous golden cave. In the rainy season the elephants lived in the cave, and in the hot weather they gathered under the branches of the banyan to enjoy the cool shade. One day the Buddha-elect with his two wives went to a grove of sal-trees, and while there he struck one of the trees with his head so that a shower of dry leaves, twigs, and red ants fell on the windward side, where his wife Chullasubhadda happened to be standing, and shower of green leaves and flowers on the other side, where his other wife, Mahasubhadda, was. On another occasion one of the elephants brought a beautiful seven-sprayed lotus to the Buddha-elect, and he received it and gave it to Mahasubhadda. Because of these things Chullasubhadda was offended and conceived a grudge against the Great Being. So one day when he had prepared an offering of fruits and flowers, and was entertaining five hundred private buddhas, Chullasubhadda also made offering to them, and made a prayer that she might be reborn as the daughter of a king and become the queen-consort of the king of Benares, and so have power to move the king to send a hunter with a poisoned arrow to wound and slay this elephant. Then she pined away and died. In due course her wicked wishes were fulfilled, and she became the favourite wife of the king of Benares, dear and pleasing in his eyes. She remembered her past lives, and said to herself that now she would have the elephant's tusks brought to her. So she went to bed and pretended to be very ill. When the king heard of this he went to her room and sat on the bed and asked her: "why are you pining away, like a wreath of withered flowers trampled under foot?" She answered: "It is because of an unattained wish;" whereupon he promised whatever she desired. So she had all the hunters of the kingdom called together, amounting to sixty thousand, and told them that she had had a dream of a magnificent six-tusked white elephant, and that if her longing for the tusks could not be satisfied she would die. She chose one of the hunters, who was a coarse, ill-favoured man, to do her work, and showed him the way to the lake where the Great Being lived, and promised him a reward of five villages when she received the tusks. He was very much afraid of the task, but finally consented when she told him that she had also dreamt that her desire would be fulfilled. She fitted him out with weapons and necessaries for the journey, giving him a leather parachute to descend from the hills to the lake.

Deeper and deeper he penetrated into the Himalayan jungle, far beyond the haunts of men, overcoming incredible difficulties, until after seven years, seven months, and seven days' weary travelling he stood by the great banyan-tree where the Buddha-elect and the other elephants lived so peacefully and unsuspectingly. He dug a hole in the ground and, putting on the yellow robe of a hermit, hid in it, covering it over except a little space for his arrow. When the Great Being passed by he shot him with a poisoned arrow, which drove him nearly mad with anger and pain. Just when he would have killed the wicked hunter he noticed his yellow robe—

Emblem of sainthood, priestly guise, And deemed inviolate by the wise.

Seeing this robe, the wounded elephant recovered his self-control and asked the hunter what reason he had for slaying him. The hunter told him his story of the dream of the queen of Benares. The Great Being understood the whole matter very well and suffered the hunter to take his tusks. But so great was he, and the hunter so clumsy, that he could not cut them away; he only gave the Great Being unbearable pain and filled his mouth with blood. Then he took the saw in his own trunk, and cut them off and gave them to the hunter, saying: "The tusks of wisdom are a hundred times dearer to me than these, and may this good act be the reason of my attaining omniscience." He also gave the hunter magic power to return to Benares in seven days, and soon died and was burned on a pyre by the other elephants. The hunter took back the tusks to

> the queen and, evidently disapproving of her wickedness now that he knew its full significance, announced that the elephant against whom she had felt a grudge for a trifling offence had been slain by him. "Is he dead?" she cried; and, giving her the tusks, "Rest assure he is dead," the hunter replied. Taking the beautiful tusks on her lap, she gazed at these tokens of one that had been her dear lord in another life, and as she gazed she was filled with inconsolable grief, and her heart broke and she died the same day.
>
> Long ages afterward she was born at Savatthi, and became a nun. She went one day with other sisters to hear the Buddha's doctrine. Gazing upon him, so peaceful and radiant, it came into her heart that she had once been his wife, when he had been lord of a herd of elephants, and she was glad. But then there came to her also the remembrance of her wickedness—how she had been the cause of his death only because of a fancied slight—and her heart grew hot within her, and she burst into tears and sobbed aloud. Then the master smiled, and when the brethren asked him why he smiled, he told this story, which hearing, many men entered on the Path, and the Sister herself afterward attained to sainthood.[2]

But most Hindus are not like the Buddha—they don't know their past lives. The texts do tell us how one might refresh one's memory in this respect, but it's a hard sell. The fact, however, that most Hindus do not recall their past lives does not prevent them, or others for that matter, from guessing. Imagining one's past life sometimes even becomes a parlor game in India.

My sister and I were meeting up after many years in Philadelphia. As we sat together catching up with our lives, in the course of which I had gotten divorced, she said simply, "You should never have married. You were a Buddhist monk in your past life, and you have resumed living like one again." That is how she psychoanalyzed my reversion to a single life. And she had studied in a convent all her life! My jaw dropped.

"Yes," I said, "but a monk who took his vows lightly, I am sure," I added with a wink. So wake up Dr. Freud—smell the coffee. You went as far as childhood. Some even go as far as the womb. And they don't go far enough.

But I have gone far enough, and I now go on to say that I was born in the city of India, once popularly known as Banaras, until that name was restored to its earlier form of Varanasi after India's independence. My memories even of this life are too confusing for me to even attempt any further retrieval.

My earliest memory of an ecstatic experience is also not spiritual. Far from it. It is literally infantile. I remember lying in a cot when I heard a kind of commotion all around me and inquired as to its cause. I was told that my cousins had come. Oh—the very cousins I remembered meeting a few months previously so fondly. I felt being buoyed up like a cork on a tide of joy.

"They have come to stay with us? For how long?"

"Forever."

I thought my heart had literally burst with joy. My chest—or whatever of it I had—I felt had exploded into bits. Then I felt reassured to discover that I was still alive.

My unbounded joy—my first remembered moment of ecstasy—had its roots in a family tragedy. I was able to piece together the entire story only when well past my teens, for we were all brought up on the filial fiction that all four of us—the three new ones and I (and then my brother and sister who succeeded me)—were all brothers and sisters born of the same parents. By the time the facts of this fiction became known to us, the fiction had become the fact.

The British were in India at the time. My paternal grandfather, a state official at the county level, was then being treated for a heart ailment. One day he was heard to say, "It seems as if everything is growing dark around me." These were his last words. My grandmother then took charge of the family.

"It must have been quite a shock," I said. At the time, she was staying in a temple she had built, and I was visiting her during my first year at the university. We got on famously.

"I will tell you a secret, my son," she said quietly, almost conspirationally. "Before I got married my father took me aside and said, 'O dear one, I have looked at the horoscopes. Be prepared. You will become widowed by your forties.' So you can say that in a sense I was expecting it."

Her two sons did well at school and rose in the ranks of the British administration. The eldest became a survey officer at Ajmer and in due course got married. It was a custom in our part of the Hindu world that, when the bride entered the house, the younger brother—in this case my father-to-be—took a peek at her. "You know," my father was to tell us in later life, "I was just a kid at the time, and yet my impression even today is one of seeing someone overwhelmingly beautiful."

Within a few years, however, my aunt lay dying of cancer of the breast. When people would ask her what would become of the three children, she would point to my mother—who had by now also become part of the household.

The end came suddenly. "Give me a picture of Shri Krishna," she had said, asking the picture of some film actress to be removed from the wall in front of her. In the meantime, my grandmother had mobilized a hymn-singing clutch of women. In the midst of the holy hymns, clutching the picture of Lord Krishna, my aunt had breathed her last.

My uncle began to plan a second marriage but sought the opinion of my father, who told him in a "brutally frank letter" (his words, I am told) that it is better not to marry but better to marry than to burn. Along with familial advice, he also sought celestial advice and consulted a famous astrologer. No one knew of these facts until after he had passed away—the account was contained in the notes found in the drawer of his table when it was cleared out after his death. The astrologer had forewarned against the danger of imminent death, and as for my uncle's designs of remarrying, the astrologer had said, "Only one wife in *dharma* (i.e. only one lawfully wedded wife) is ordained." My uncle had gone on a trip and returned with a fever. It developed into blood poisoning. My father could hear his brother's heart beat as he entered the hospital room. One shot of penicillin would have cured him, but penicillin was reserved for use by the army alone. The Second World War was on.

This was the chain of events, which had brought my new brothers and sisters to live with us, which had made my heart leap with such joy.

When the servant would carry me out for an outing on his shoulders, I can even now remember the funeral *ghats* burning on the banks of the Ganges in Banaras. If I knew then what I know now, I would have repeated the lines of the Nepali poet:

> Despise not the dead.
> They keep Banaras aflame.

It is said that one who dies in Benaras goes to Shiva's paradise. The more relevant question from my point of view of course was: what happens to those who are born in Banaras?

Read on.

Nainital

It has been famously asked, "If I can recall my past, why can't I recall my future?" I wish to begin by asking, "If I can change my future, why can't I change my past?"

In a sense, of course, we do it all the time. Every time we talk of our past we have moved farther away from it, so our focus on it changes. Indeed, it is changing ever so imperceptibly but definitely even as I write this. Thus, not only does our focus on the past invariably change; how we filter it in the present also changes variably—depending on what we choose to talk about—our life at home, at school or on the playground, the bench or at the shrine. . . .

It is this last filter through which I will have my past approach me this time. I must have been six- or seven-years-old. This shrine is a domestic shrine. It is a corner of the living room where I see the colorful lives of our gods in polychrome, in the dim light of the flickering candle in a cosy room in a large building atop a mountain. There is this being depicted on the shelf: it has four arms, with each arm bearing a different object. I remember the lotus, clearly a form of self-indulgence. But there is the conch shell too. I am told they are found on the ocean shores. What's an ocean?

I am roused from the reverie by the stentorian call of my mother. "Children. Line up before the images. Follow the instructions of the priest." Oh, he is the same person who tells us those wonderful stories at bedtime. "Recite after me," he says and begins to sing, in a singsong way. This must have been a routine of some standing for me to remember the lines even now:

> You are my father and my mother
> You are my relative and my friend

> You are my learning and my wealth
> You are all that I have, from beginning to end.

I was to learn in later life that this hymn—as popular all over India as it is simple—was composed by Sri Ramanujacarya, one of the great philosopher-devotees of Hinduism. Then, I knew what it meant but not what it said; now I know what it says, but do I know what it means? Spiritual progress is not always linear.

"Now, touch the feet of your mother and go to sleep. Don't fail to pray to God and ask him for what you want. God gives us all that we need."

I was yet to learn that God perhaps gives you what you need not what you want—not always anyway. And I had yet to learn that a quicker way of getting what you want was by going after it and getting it—rather than asking God for it. He takes too much time to deliver. And sometimes he does not deliver at all.

We slipped under the covers, and I said my prayer: "God, please grant me two things: that I may have a vision of you (I visualized him with four arms with all the objects they held in my mind as I said this) and that I may stand first in my class at school."

Years later, I was reading *Talks with Sri Ramana Maharshi*. Ramana Maharshi, who died in 1950, is considered one of modern India's great sages. Suddenly, I came across a passage in which he seemed to be poking fun at me. It read in effect: "Some people think that when they will have a vision of God they will see him standing before them, holding various things in his arm. . . ."

I began to squirm as I read this. But I read on:

> . . . as if he will be carrying various objects in his hand. . . .[1]

My ears began to burn. I no longer had the benefit of the innocence of childhood to save me from the embarrassment of having actually thought that this is what God's vision would be like.

God's vision, in whatever form, is still on hold, but I did start standing first in my class—but that came years later, when I stopped praying and started studying.

I now consider it striking that, the earliest thing I can remember praying for, was the vision of God. Does our culture capture us *that* early in life?

* * *

I still remember what a glorious morning it was as the child brigade—that's how the five of us were called—was summoned outdoors.

"Look, look. Nanda Devi." And out at a distance, far away like a distant divinity, there stood this brilliant peak. It was called Nanda Devi. Even though a child takes only small breaths, it was breathtaking.

"Quick, quick. Look through the binoculars."

It must have been one of those wonderful moments of childhood, which makes being a child such a romance. The peak still stood before us—only magnified. And what was this I was seeing—troopers on horses marching single file, all crisply dressed with banners fluttering away. Was this just my imagination? No—others confirmed the sighting, and we had public verification of reality. Only in later life would even this mode of verification be thrown into doubt—do all of us see the *same* tree?

Such are the nirvanas of one's childhood.

When was I first told that the Himalayas are the playground of the gods? I don't know when I was first told so, but when I first knew so was when I saw Nanda Devi.

I was told that the place we were living at the time was called Nainital, named after the mountainous lake (Tal), around which it was built. It was as beautiful a place as can be—one to make one catch one's breath. Around the lake was a rider's path, which we would follow either on foot or on horse. Once peering into waters, I asked the escort, "How deep is it?"

"No one knows. The British brought their special equipment but could not get to the bottom of it. It is fathomless. It goes to the other world."

What other world could there be, I remember thinking to myself? And who are the British? But already I was beginning to look upon them as a technically proficient and technologically advanced people—even though they could not get to the bottom of the lake.

Our house lay at the mountain top. During the day, we would often come down to the lake, and as the evening shadows lengthened, we would have to scamper all the way to the top. One day, the trip became memorable as we crunched over dried leaves on our way up. There was a sudden rustling of the leaves, and we were warned to stop at once in an alarmed tone. The rustling went like an ripple through the leaves, leaving us both transfixed and dumbfounded. Then someone hissed, "That was a snake." We were all made to march single file by the priest, who then guided us to the top. "God Shiva, can deal with them," he muttered, "we mortals can't."

Now, if someone were to ask me when did I first begin to believe in God, or in Vishnu, or in the Devi, or Shiva—what can I tell him or her? Do I know?

Some years later when I was more of a boy and less of a child, Nainital would figure in my life once more. But all that I remember are these few scenes.

There is this long arched pathway of stone, and two nuns are talking, rosaries in hand. As I approach, then I begin to think: we have been told always to say "excuse me" if we go past someone on a narrow path, and the person has to make way for us. I would usually follow these instructions, but I was feeling mischievous today. So I say to myself, "They are immersed in conversation so let me sneak past them. No one would be the wiser." So I do. And now I am so far out on my way that I think I have gotten away with it and am about to congratulate myself for it, when I hear a voice calling my name, and this makes my heart sink. "Go all the way up from where you came and come down again and go past us saying what you have to say!"

Later on, although I don't know anything about Christianity, I learnt my religion had a word for it. It is called karma.

About the same time, I remember us standing in front of an altar, wearing special clothes. And then chanting in a language I don't understand (it was Latin), and then we are all made to kneel as we go past a picture of a person laid out on a cross. That is after we have crossed our chest with our hands in a certain way, making certain sounds. This went on for a few days.

Then one day, just before the session was about to begin, some of us were asked to leave the lineup. These "some" soon become many, then most. We are all now sitting or standing on a knoll waiting, as the other boys went through the same ritual we used to. Then, after they were done, we joined them, and everything was back to normal.

This mystery can now be cleared up. The Indian government had issued instructions that non-Christian students studying in Christian institutions were to be exempted from attending Christian rites. This is how the law translated into practice.

I remember my mother coming to visit me when I was there. I remember asking her insistently:

> "Who am I?"
>
> "What do you mean who am I?"
>
> "Well, that playmate of mine says he is Belgian; this other mate says he is British."

"You are an Indian!" my mother told me, giving me a lingering look.

She still remembers me saying to myself, "I am an Indian. I am an Indian. I am an Indian."

So, although I don't know when I came to know I was a Hindu, I do know the precise moment I discovered I was an Indian!

But soon there was trouble in paradise. I had mentioned earlier that Nainital was so beautiful as to make me catch my breath. It made me catch mine once too often. I was diagnosed as asthmatic, and the damp climate of Nainital seemed to make it worse. So, one day I found myself suddenly traveling down from the mountains to the plains. I had to be recalled from the convent, where my sisters continued to study.

It was an uneventful journey until we were close to our destination. Reaching our destination involved crossing a river. I was joining my family in Fatehpur, as my stay at the Nainital convent had been aborted on medical grounds. Even crossing the river was routine until I spied some people sitting by the banks, who seemed to be simply waiting.

"What are they doing?" I asked my companion.
"Waiting for the fish to bite at the bait."
"What do they do when that happens."
"Reel them in and kill them. Then they eat them."

I was shocked speechless for a while. When my vocal chords were ready to function again, I asked, "But why? Can't they eat bread? Why kill something to eat?"

From the way he dismissed my remark, I gathered that it was not as acute a moral issue for him as it had become for me at the time.

The rest of my boat ride across the river was torture. I would look around frantically, and as the bait would dip, my heart would sink, and I would pray, "O God, please spare this fish. Please spare its life."

Today, I wonder: how and when did I form this mental impression—or *saṁskāra* as we Hindus call them—that I should not take life and certainly not just to have lunch? Was I was already a vegetarian without knowing it?

So I left behind the world of Nainital. And then a few years ago, Nainital entered my world once again in a way difficult to anticipate. I was preparing a presentation for the class on Hindu thought at McGill University. We had now entered the period of modern Hinduism. Whereas classical Hindu thought flows along the accustomed channels of the established schools of Hindu philosophy, modern Hindu thought breaks this pattern, inasmuch as its nodal points are not schools of thought but individual thinkers. The lives of the classical thinkers—while hagiographically enticing, are autobiographically short on personal details. But I could, I thought, do better with modern Hindu thinkers, such as Vivekananda, whose lives are amply documented by their followers in the East and West. In my attempt, I came across the following entry by Sister Nivedita, a well-known disciple of Swami Vivekananda, in her Notes on Some Wandering from May, 14 to 16, 1898:

> May, 14 to 16
>
> Naini Tal was made beautiful by three things,—the Master's pleasure in introducing to us his disciple, the Raja of Khetri; the *dancing girls* who met us and asked us where to find him, in spite of the remonstrances of others; and by the Mohammedan gentleman who said, "Swamiji, if in aftertimes any claim you as an Avatar, remember that I, a Mohammedan, am the first!"
>
> It was here, too, that we heard a long talk on Ram Mohun Roy, in which he pointed out three things as the dominant notes of this teacher's message, his acceptance of the Vedanta, his preaching of patriotism, and the love that embraced the Mussulman equally with the Hindu. In all these things, he claimed himself to have taken up the task that breadth and foresight of Ram Mohun Roy had mapped out.
>
> The incident of the dancing girls occurred in consequence of our visit to the two temples at the head of the tarn, which from time immemorial have been places of pilgrimage, making the beautiful little "Eye Lake" holy. Here, offering worship, we found two nautch-women. When they had finished, they came up to us, and we in broken language, entered into conversation with them. We took them for respectable ladies of the town, and were much astonished, later, at the storm which had evidently passed over the Swami's audience at his refusal to have them turned away. Am I mistaken in thinking that it was in connection with these dancing-women of Naini Tal that he first told

us the story, many times repeated, of the nautch-girl of Khetri? He had been angry at the invitation to see her, but being prevailed upon to come, she sang—

"O Lord, look not upon my evil qualities!
Thy name, O Lord, is Same-sightedness,
Make us both the same Brahman!
One piece of iron is the knife in the hand of the butcher,
And another piece of iron is in the image in the temple.
But when they touch the philosopher's stone,
Both alike turn to gold!
One drop of water is in the sacred Jamuna,
And one is foul in a ditch by the roadside.
But when they fall into the Ganges,
Both alike become holy!
So, Lord, look not upon my evil qualities!
Thy name, O Lord, is Same—Sightedness.
Make us both the same Brahman!"

And then, said the Master of himself, the scales fell from his eyes, and seeing that all are indeed one, he condemned no more.[2]

Thus do the haunts of our childhood come back to haunt us, but not as in witchcraft but as in Wicca.

Fatehpur

It was a huge house we dwelt in. It was approached by a winding and dusty road with hectares sprawled around it. Is it true that this was a punitive posting for my father for having dueled verbally with the chief minister of the province, who was elected to power under an installment of self-government, offered by the British as a sop to the rising tide of Indian nationalism?

I was too young for this world of professional reprisals but too old to be left without religious roots. A story heard years later in a class of Professor Wilfred Cantwell Smith seems anachronistically relevant. After Islam had came to Persia, Ibn Mukaffa, a prominent Zoroastrian, decided to convert to it. He was a person of sufficient stature for the event that was to take place the next morning to be considered a public one. That previous night, however, he was observed performing the Zoroastrian verspertine rituals by his friends, who expressed surprise that he should be doing so when come next day he was going to convert to Islam. He is believed to have responded to the sceptical thrust of their statement with the following remark: "One should never go to bed without a religion."

I doubt if my parents had heard of this justification, but they had probably intuited the sentiment.

I was now going to be taught how to perform the Hindu fire-ceremony (*havana*). It was done in the open. A special receptacle was placed in front and filled with various combustible items. I was made to sip water ceremonially, while rings of a special kind of grass were slipped into my fingers. Then, the fire was lit, and at specified intervals, I poured oblations into it to the utterance of "*svāhā*." Soon the holy smoke spread in all directions, invading the building as well. The *saṁkalpa*, which I then recited mechanically, I was to find fascinating intellectually when I became a student of religion. This declaratory formula locates one in the sacred time and space of the Hindu world. As the noted authority P.V. Kane points out:

> In the Sankalpa (declaratory formula) for every religious ceremony the performer has to mention the grand divisions and sub-divisions of time beginning with Śvetavarāhakalpa, such as Vaivasvata manvantara, Kaliyuga and its first quarter together with the geographical position of the place of performance in Bharatavarṣa, and the Zodiacal signs occupied by the Sun, Jupiter and other planets, the era, name of year (Jovian), the month, the fortnight, the tithi, nakṣatra, Yoga and Karaṇa. A verse of Devala states that if a man performing a religious rite does not mention the month, the fortnight, the tithi and the occasion (of the rite) he will not reap the merit of the rite. That is the importance of eras, years and its sub-divisions in the religious life of our people. Therefore a calendar (pañcāṅga) is absolutely necessary for every religious Hindu.[1]

The great savant understates the point. A geographical statement of matching minutae also forms part of it. The dead bones of these academic pronouncements take on vital life as I remember sitting there chanting: . . . *jambudvīpe bharatakhaṇḍe āryāvarte*. . . . the words to the accompaniment of which oblations are made: "In the continent called Jambudvīpa, in the part known as Bharatakhaṇḍa, in the region known as Āryāvarta . . ."

I did not quite know what I was doing, but perhaps culture consists in sharing knowledge without knowing precisely what it is.

I remember my mother remarking how purified and holy everything felt after the rite had been performed. If the sanctification of our life, and our actions in life, is one purpose of ritual, then it had been fulfilled.

The liturgical aspect of this ritual consisted of the recitation of the *gāyatrī* (the verse from the Ṛg Veda [111.6.2.10] with which one is initiated into Vedic studies). For some reason, my memory of the ritual is visual and aural rather than oral—in the sense that I do not remember the mantra being transmitted to me, but it must have been. Similarly, I have only a very vague recall of the sacred thread, although I must have donned that also. The wearing of the sacred thread indicates that one has been initiated into Vedic studies.

It was also around this time that I began to feel devotional stirrings. The Hindu pantheon offers one a lot to choose from. The figure of Rāma evoked my admiration: his valor, his steadfastness, his devotion to Sītā, or what one would now describe as his "family values"—made a great impression on me. I now suspect that his appeal may have been as literary as religious, for I found listening to the discourses on Tulsīdās's *Rāmacaritamānas* totally enrapturing. Shall we say that I entered the magic chamber of devotional Hinduism through the portal of Rāma?

The mesmeric poetic recitation of the text is incapable of being captured in prose; there can be no substitutes for it, and if there are substitutes for it, then they can only range from poor to poorer. Nevertheless, here's an attempt. It is part of the epic narrative that the demon-king Rāvaṇa abducts Sītā, the wife of Rāma, in his aerial car (whose description as Rāvaṇa's private jet amuses my classes no end). While she was, thus, being carried away, a chivalrous vulture, having divined the demon's nefarious intent, tried to prevent the abduction of Sītā. The attempt was futile; he fell to the ground mortally wounded and lay there awaiting his end. In the meantime Rāma, and his brother Lakṣmaṇa, were roaming the jungle in search of the missing Sītā and finally found "the vulture-king lying, with his thoughts fixed on the prints of Rāma's feet." The account of Tulsīdās continues as follows:

> The compassionate Raghubir laid his lotus hands upon his head. At the sight of Rama's lovely face all his pain was forgotten, and the vulture recovered himself and spoke as follows: "Hearken Rama, remover of life's troubles. My lord, this is Ravan's doing, he is the wretch, who has carried off Janak's daughter. He took her away, sire, to the south, crying as piteously as an osprey. I have kept alive, my lord, only to see you; now, O most merciful, I would depart." Said Rama: "Remain alive, father." He smiled and answered: "He, by the repetition of whose name at the hour of death the vilest sinner, as the scriptures declare, attains salvation, has come in bodily form before my eyes; what need is there, sire, for me to live any longer?" Raghubir's eyes filled with tears as he replied: "Father, it is your own good deeds that have saved you. There is nothing in the world beyond the reach of those who devote their soul to the good of others. When you pass out of the body, father,

> ascend to my sphere in heaven. What more can I give you? Your every wish is gratified."[2]

A good reciter can keep an audience spellbound for entire evenings over a period of several days merely expounding on this incident. But my devotion for Rāma and his entourage did not extend to my sisters, who, when at home on vacation from the convent, would poke fun at the monkey-faced god Hanumān, often depicted with Rāma as his loyal devotee.

Delhi

Life took on a deeper hue once we moved to Delhi. I was entering the teens, beginning to play cricket and waking up to the world around me.

By now, the problem of the apparent injustices of life had begun to appear on the horizon. It did not assume an acute shape, but it did begin to appear in the form of a mild puzzle. The reason was not far to seek. We were a family of seven kids now. I did not mention this earlier, but it needs to be mentioned now that my eldest brother was deaf and mute. It was perhaps only now, as we grew up, that the awareness of what it meant began to dawn on me. Our eldest brother existed normally but on the margins of the household. He kept himself preoccupied with his own pastimes—sketching being one of them. But the fact that he could not be one of us was apparent, and this raised the obvious question: Why? Why this difference (brought on by an attack of meningitis in childhood)?

Once, while we were at the hill station of Nainital, he was found missing, and a frantic search was mounted. He was used to making a distinct, if to us, meaningless sound. He had been lost for the evening. Night came in upon us. The search was on. Then, in the stillness of the night, when we were on the point of giving up, his oral signature was heard from deep down in the valley. A party rushed down and found him scraped but safe at the bottom of the hill. He had apparently ventured too far on the ledge of the slope in search of berries and had fallen.

Nor was this all. In later life, he developed epilepsy. So, on the edge of our lives hung this question mark: why should he be singled out for such "punishment"? In his early twenties, he suffered a fatal seizure. I remember the occasion well because I was immersed in undergraduate studies, trying my best to make the grade. It was around the time my eldest sister had her first child and was visiting us. It was she who drew our attention to his condition in the morning. I remember well the glazed look of death, which I was seeing for the first time in my life.

There were other indications of the contingent nature of things, less wrenching but nevertheless disturbing. I had myself barely avoided being electrocuted to death as a toddler. My mother's presence of mind had saved my life. I had also, more providentially, been saved in the nick of time from being run over by an oncoming train. I was with my mother on one side of the railway platform, hanging on to her hand as small children do, when I saw my father on the other side. The impulse to be with my father made me struggle myself free from my mother's hand and dart across to the opposite side of the platform. The only problem was that it was easy to get down on one side, but as I tried to clamber up the other side, I could not. I remember making one try and failing, and then another try and failing—and, then suddenly, I found a hand stretched out toward me from nowhere. I clutched at it and clambered onto the other side—but, as I did, I heard the engine speed past me, and this left me wondering, "Was I that close?"

In the commotion, my mother had no idea what had happened. I suddenly heard people shouting, "Show him to the mother; show him to the mother." The incoming train stopped in the meantime. I was hoisted on a shoulder and carried past the vision–blocking train, so that my mother could know I was safe.

I shall never forget the look on her face.

By now I had also become aware of other incidents, one of which involved my father. The incident took place again in the hill station of Nainital on a dark and stormy night, as my father was making his way up the hill to our house. The disturbed metereological conditions had disoriented my father to the point that he started walking diagonally off the pathway toward the gorge, instead of moving forward on the path. With one more step, he would have fallen into the gorge—but for a sky-shattering bolt of lightning, which froze him in place. He said he saw his entire life flash past at that moment. Then gingerly, hugging the hill, he made his way back home.

How did I account for these phenomena? Although by no means an atheist, I am now struck by the fact that I rarely connected these two experiences with God. The explanation of choice for me was not chance either but rather karma. Karma is of course a complex and multivalent concept, but somehow it seemed to provide enough of an explanation for me to sustain a coherent vision of the world. Even in later life, when I encountered such incidents, my confidence in karma as an explanation reminded intact.

But what is karma? Perhaps this tale will make it clear:

There was a Seth [wealthy proprietor; merchant]. The Seth's name was Nagpal.

[We laugh, for Nagpal is a wealthy industrialist known to most visitors. "Not your Bombay Nagpal," Swamiji assures. "Yes?"]

He lived in Ujjain. He was a very wealthy Seth. He built many houses.

["Did you hear this story?" Swamiji looks around through his glasses. Heads shake: No. Swamiji resumes, the smile broadening on his face.]

He built a house, a house that was very beautiful. He called in many skilled craftsmen. There was no other house like this in Ujjain. After building this house, there was still a little work left before it was completed. Just one or two days of work were left. Statues had been made all over the house: statues. Many statues had been made. They all had to be painted. Then he was telling the craftsmen, "Look brothers, this house, my house, has turned out beautifully. No one in Ujjain has a house like this. Even the government doesn't have buildings like this."

Those people said [respectfully], "This is true, Maharaj."

"As you paint these, give them the kind of color that will last for seven generations. It should appear very beautiful. For seven generations!

[Kirin has been waiting for Swamiji to finish the last few lines before she translates, but he turns to her clarifying the Hindi pirha with the English word "relation." "Generation!" amends Kirin. Swamiji nods, his attention flicking from her back into the plot.]

"It should stay that beautiful. Just as he was finishing saying this, a Babaji like our Sadananda arrived there.

[Sandananda's eyebrows lift and he grins. He is a long-limbed, bearded man on the verge of middle age, with an ochre cloth wrapped around his waist.]

He arrived there and saw them just as the King was finishing what he said. Not the king, the Seth. [Swamiji hastily corrects, "The Seth, the Seth."] The Sadhu witnessed this. He laughed. He laughed inside his mind. Then he walked away.

The Seth saw him. "Why did this Maharaj laugh? What does this Babaji know? Babajis only know how to eat off other people! [We laugh.] What does he know about this house? He just laughed for no reason. He doesn't even know how to wear proper clothes!" ["Bhavani" lets out a chortle, possibly because Swamiji himself can be somewhat "topsy-turvy" in his appearance.] He kept quiet. But it stuck in his mind, "What did I do wrong? Why did he laugh?"

Then, he had a shop, a big shop. In the morning, he would give work to everyone and then go sit in the shop. He went there and sat down [Swamiji sneezes, then resumes,] and as he sat . . . his business went on, tens of thousands of rupees of business. In front of him, all his employees packed things up; they filled trucks of goods: all this went on. The Seth was sitting inside. There was a space for the Seth to sit and he was sitting there. He was keeping track of the cash.

Just then a goat, you know, came running up to the Seth. He came and stood close to him. Behind him was a man who slaughters goats: a butcher. ["Slaughter" echoes Gupta Seth, addressing himself to Kirin]. He came in, too. He said, "Seth, this is my goat, and I was taking him to be slaughtered. He slipped out of my hands and came up to you. Just push him out please. I want him to be slaughtered."

It came into the Seth's mind, "This goat has come to me. It's my job to save his life. Then, too, I am so rich." He asked the butcher, "How much does this goat cost? Let him go and I'll give you the money."

He said, "Maharaj, give me fifteen gold coins [mohur] for him."

[Kirin blithely mistranslates gold coin (mohur) as peacock (mor). "Mohur, mohur," corrects Meena Gupta grinning from beside Kirin. "Not peacock!" says Gupta Saheb in English. "What's a mohur, Swamiji?" Kirin asks in confusion. "Gold coin," Gupta Saheb explains. "Not just gold," Swamiji explains. "When you say one mohur you mean about four rupees. So fifteen mohur means sixty rupees. Yes?"]

"Give me that much money, and I'll leave the goat for you," he said.

It's a habit of Seths to think, "Why fifteen gold coins for a goat?"

[Amusement ripples from the Indians listening, for merchants are proverbially stingy]. He said, "I'll give you fourteen gold coins for him." If you say ten rupees, it's their habit to say five![“They want to negotiate," Gupta Saheb clarifies in English].

The Seth said fourteen. The butcher said, "Maharaj you won't get him for fourteen. There's fifteen rupees worth of mutton in this goat: fifteen gold coins. I bought him just after weighing him. If I slaughter him and sell the flesh, it's worth sixty rupees. That is rightfully mine. Now if you give me that much, I'll give him to you. Otherwise I can't give him to you." He said this once.

"Fourteen," said the Seth. Then he thought: Whose goat is this anyways, and why pay money for him?" He didn't want to give even fourteen rupees. [We know Swamiji means mohur, but no one corrects him. We laugh again for the Seth is acting up to the tight-fisted stereotype.] "I don't want to slaughter this or anything else: what do I have to do with this goat? Why waste money for no reason?" So he thought, "Somehow I should take back my words." He said, "If you want to give him to me for fourteen mohur then hand him over, otherwise take your goat away."

He said, "I won't give him up for fourteen mohur, if you won't pay fifteen, give back the goat."

He said, "Fine. Take your goat away." He grabbed the goat by the ears and handed him over like this [Swamiji extends both hands.].

As he was handing him over, just then the Babaji came up in front of him. The Babaji saw him doing this. The Babaji looked at him and laughed. As he was handing him over [Swamiji's hands are frozen in front of him and his head turns towards Sadananda.], he saw the Babaji. The Babaji was laughing. He thought, "I've seen the Babaji again, what's going on? The Babaji is laughing." Then he remained silent. The Babaji went off.

Then after doing all his business, the Seth went home around twelve or one o'clock. That day it was one year since his child was born. He had just one son. For a long time, he had no children.

His wife was waiting for her husband to return. She had made nice food. It was a year since the child's birth. ["Burtha-day" Swamiji explains in English. "Bhavani" lets out a low, delighted chuckle.] As the husband was coming, she had set out a silver plate [thali]. When he saw his father, the baby wiggled his head like this—"Swamiji bobs in his seat, shaking his shoulders, rolling his head]—the baby who was sitting in his mother's lap. She had made all kinds of preparations, was doing all kinds of things, had set out lots of fine sweets. She served sweets, she served fried bread [puri], she served all kinds of good things to eat. He was eating.

The baby was sitting in his mother's lap, wiggling his head, jumping around. [Swamiji demonstrates: an oversized infant wearing ochre. Watching him, it is impossible not to laugh.] He was jumping, the way babies do, pushing up straight [hunching his back, then suddenly flexing it; arms raised from the elbows and clenched at the fists]. When his mother saw this, she said, "Look how happy this child is when he sees you!"

He said [reaching out his hands], "Give him to me!" He sat the baby down in his lap.

"Now you too feed him a bite or two since he's one year old," she said. So he also puts a bit of those sweets into the baby's mouth. [Left elbow crooked as though supporting the baby, Swamiji thrusts the bunched fingers of his right hand toward it.] It was a baby. You have love for a baby don't you? Just then—it's a baby's habit—he let out a stream of pee—chulllll! [Swamiji flings out his hand to show how far the pee went. Along with him, we are all hopelessly laughing.] When he peed, it fell all over his father's clothes. "Che-che, he's peed!" he did this [distastefully flicking and wiping at his robes, then swiftly depositing the imaginary bundle over the edge of the chair!]. When babies pee, you know, they pee quite a distance! Some fell on the plate, too. "What has this baby done peeing?" he said.

His wife said, "So what if he peed, he's your own child." She took the baby back.

Then he was sitting there eating from that very plate. The food that had been peed on was on one side, and he was eating from that very side. Not too much pee, just a little had fallen on the food.

Just then, once again the Babaji appeared. "Give me alms, [bhavati bhiksham dehi] he called. Yes? The Seth heard this as he was eating. It was the same Babaji. The Babaji was laughing from over there.

Then he couldn't endure this in his mind. "I've seen him three times today, and all three times this Babaji has laughed! I must have made some kind of mistake, and that's why this Babaji is laughing. There seems to be some secret on his lips." So he immediately left his food. He went and prostrated at the Babaji's feet. "Babaji, what's going on? I've had darshan of you three times. I'm very fortunate to have done so. All three times you laughed; there seems to be some secret hidden in your lips. You're not saying anything. Why do you laugh, what is the reason? Tell me, what did I do wrong?"

He said, "It's nothing, ji. We sadhus are always laughing."

"No, no. There's something or the other in your laughter. You'll have to tell me."

He said, "If you want me to tell you why, you must come alone in the evening to the banks of the Sipra river. ["The Sipra river in Ujjain," Swamiji adds as an aside.] Come, and I'll tell you: at five o'clock."

"Fine," the Seth said.

He went there at exactly five o'clock. Talking away, the two of them walked some distance along the river bank. When they reached a deserted place, the Seth caught hold of the Babaji's feet. "Now tell me, why did you laugh?"

The Babaji said, "Forget about it, ji, why do you ask about everything? I just laughed for no particular reason."

"No, no, you must tell me something."

"What's this about? What should I tell you? Ask me."

He said, "This morning, as I was telling the employees to paint the statues. At that time, you looked at me, laughed, and went away. You didn't say anything, you just looked, laughed and left. What was the reason for this?"

[I'll give you a banana, Doctor Sahib," Swamiji motions to the doctor's youngest son who had come in with his lunch and is now slipping out the door. "I'll give you a nice banana." He breaks one from the bunch and hands it over as he continues speaking].

The Babaji said, "Look, it's like this. What I specially saw was the great hopes a soul [jiv] has. You're going to die in seven days. You're thinking about seven generations. After you die, how does what becomes of the house matter to you? Why are you worrying about seven generations now? When I saw this, it made me laugh. He'll die in seven days and he's thinking about seven generations!"

"Will I die in seven days?!" [Eyes widening in alarm.]

"Oh, yes!" [Swamiji's droll enunciation of English makes us all—especially the Westerners—laugh.]

"All right, ji, let's forget that." [Swamiji's voice drops into a mumbling, worried, undertone, hand to his chin.] We sit silent. There is a pause, and then his voice gathers strength for the next question. "Then, when I was sitting in the shop and handing over the goat; at that time you laughed. Why was this?"

"Forget that, ji, forget it," he said.

The Seth said, "You have to tell me that, too."

"Do you know who that goat is?" he asked.

"Who is he?"

"He's your father," the Babaji said.

"My father!" [Swamiji stares with alarm. Another wave of laughter breaks over the room.]

He said, "That butcher was a porter before. Your father told a lie about sixty rupees, he wrote this off and embezzled it from him; he wrote false accounts. Your father did a bad thing with this money when he embezzled it. Then your father died. When he died, according to his past actions (karma) he took birth as a goat. Then, the man who had been a porter couldn't earn enough and started working as a butcher instead. Now your father was a goat. He had to repay the money; the goat was caught. He had to repay the money, right? What does a goat have? His mutton would have to be sold. 'I gave my children great riches. My child will release me.': he thought this and came to you."

[Here Kirin's tape snapped to the end, and, turning it over, she missed recording the next line: "The butcher asked for fifteen gold coins but you only want to give fourteen."]

"If you had only given the fifteenth gold coin your father would have been saved. You were miserly about four rupees, though you have eaten so much of his wealth—just because of four rupees you couldn't save your father. He had to give his mutton to free himself of the debt. [Swamiji laughs low, amusement bubbling between his words.] By dying, he could return the debt. It was paid off."

And the third thing the Seth asked was, "When I was at home, why did you laugh? The time I was eating my food."

He said, "Just forget about that, ji."

"No, you must tell me that, too."

"Do you know who your child is? Do you know why your child looked at you and laughed?

He said, "What is it?"

"That child was your wife's lover in the past. He loved her. You had money in hand, you had him murdered. To get his revenge this man took birth as your child, in your house. You killed him then, and now he sits on your wife's lap! When he sees you, he wiggles his head, he laughs. [Laughter—especially from the women.] 'Now, what will you do to me? I sit here with such authority. Watch, I'll show you. You've talked about seven generations; in one generation I'll ruin your name. I'll make your name a bad name. I'll finish off all your wealth.' The child looks at you saying this. Then as you sit and feed him—you eat off a silver plate, right?—he says. 'Eat my piss' and he pees. [Laughter shakes the room.] You feed him with love. When I saw this, it made me laugh. You couldn't save your father because of four rupees; your enemy pees and you eat it! Thinking about the ways of the world, I laughed. No one knows what lies ahead. The Lord's play is strange and marvelous [ajab]. This is what made me laugh."

He said [brow laden with worry], "Will I really die in seven days?"

"You'll certainly die."

"How will I die?"

"You'll have a sharp pain in your head. [Kirin hesitates while translating and Swamiji proffers in English "head-ache!"] You'll die because of this."

"If this is so, then what should I do?"

"Since this is so, you should divide your riches into four portions. One portion should be given to the poor.

> One portion should be kept for your wife and child. One portion should be given to a temple or a mosque. And one portion should be given to some friend or old person. Then this will all be of use to you. You'll definitely die."
>
> That story is now finished.[1]

Such stories almost cheerfully explain the vagaries of our life in terms of karma. But sometimes the question is forced on us so acutely that the explanation almost buckles.

This happened when we were living in Agra. I was about to come out of my teens at the time and had spent several years in academic endeavor.

While we were in Delhi. I had acquired a sister, the youngest. I remember my mother going for a medical checkup and returning somewhat shocked that she was pregnant! My sister must have been around nine at the time. We were now living in Agra.

I went to bed as on any other day, but when I woke up, it was not like any other day. My youngest sister was in the hospital fighting for her life.

In the night, she had complained of a headache, and my brother tried to comfort her. By the time my parents returned from the party they were out to, she was running such a high fever that she had to be rushed to the hospital.

All this seemed like a nightmare, but a distant nightmare, as I went about my daily business in the hope that the crisis would pass, although the ailment had been diagnosed as cerebral meningitis.

Then I received word that my presence was urgently required. As soon as I entered the room, I realized that my optimism had been an utter delusion. My sister lay in a coma, virtually naked with all kinds of medical appurtenances going in and coming out of her. My mother asked me to go into a corner and repeat the *trayambaka* mantra. This is a mantra in honor of Shiva and was believed to possess life-saving properties. I retired to the corner and dutifully complied. While I was, thus, engaged, I saw my sister momentarily come out of the coma—peering in the dark, crying "Mummy, Mummy." "Yes dear, I am here," said my mother, choking, holding her hand. Then, my sister suddenly went back into the coma.

I think she had lost her sight by that time.

She never recovered and passed away within hours.

The mantra had made no difference at least this time. We were utterly heartbroken.

When the body was being prepared up to be taken out to the cremation ground, my mother dressed her as a princess. My brother broke down completely. I somehow managed to retain a detached manner. Others grieved in one big moment—my grief came out in fragments of verse I wrote from time to time. Everyone copes with life, or death, in their own way.

Just at that moment my maternal grandmother arrived, totally unannounced. She saw this scene and cursed God, "Do we produce children to make offerings of them to you?"

A few weeks before all this happened, my sister had told my mother what she has just read in the *Bhagavadgītā*, "Just as a person casts off worn-out garments and puts on new ones, we cast off old bodies and acquire new ones."

After a few days my mother told me, "Remember the astrologer who used to live around the house in Delhi who had migrated from Sindh—after Partition?"

"The one who said the ceiling of the room I was born in must have caved in?" "Yes," she said. "When he cast your sister's horoscope, he said, 'Do not become too attached to her until she is well past her ninth year.' " This is how predictions of mortality are coded in India.

"She was just nine," my mother said. "Almost. I had just begun to hope that perhaps we are in the clear now."

The astrologer's mention brings up the question of theodicy in a way really hard to handle. The division of the subcontinent into India and Pakistan cost at least half a million lives and uprooted another fourteen million. It is, thus, somewhat akin to the Jewish Holocaust, which was on a scale all its own. But let us turn from millions to just one human being.

A big road ran past our house, and a hutment abutted on it next to our house. The astrologer used to live there with a friend or colleague, who set up his small shop every morning and eked out a living in this way. We, as children, would sometimes go out and tease him. One day we went too far. He just folded up his shop and went back into the house on the verge of tears, as we were having fun at his expense.

Within an hour or so, we were hauled up before our mother. We were severely rebuked and asked to leave him severely alone—or else. Her dressing down was peppered with words like "India," "Pakistan," "British," "Partition," "Refugee," "a big businessman who had to flee because he was a Hindu . . ." and so on. The content of what she said we couldn't understand then; the tone we understood only too well. I still remember the smile on his face when we cravenly apologized to him.

Then, we knew nothing. Now, we know only too well. Alas! There is no way to go back in time and make full amends. Put that down to karma. But whose?

The Hindu World

I

By the time I emerged from my teens, the key elements constituting the kaleidoscope of Hinduism were now within the tube. There was the doctrine of karma and rebirth, which I imbibed early—as also the emphasis on truth and nonviolence, quite consistent with the above doctrines for it was the moral quality of one's life, which determined its karmic quality. God was present as the center of my devotion. It was not the God of the philosophers but of the worshippers. I had gained some familiarity with the rites and rituals of Hinduism and even spent some time in a temple, but I had acquired enough acquaintance with Buddhism to be skeptical of Hinduism!

But what about the nature of the ultimate reality?

For finding the building blocks of the universe, my quarry was Vedanta.

I first became aware of the word through my utter ignorance of it. At the time, I was a student in Delhi, and the school advertised classes in French for those who would wish to take them after regular hours. I am not quite sure of my motive in embarking on a stint of learning French. But, for me, a curious development occurred at the end of one of these sessions. Our French teacher turned to us and said:

Does anyone of you know anything about Vedanta?

I could now say, with the benefit of hindsight, that he was perhaps in India on a spiritual quest.

It was a group of about half a dozen students. I do not know why, but all eyes turned in my direction.

It was an elusive moment which followed. Here was a word I had vaguely heard but had no idea what it stood for, and yet there was this inner monitor telling me that I should know what it meant. But in the end I decided to tell the bare truth and said, "No. Know nothing about it."

In some indescribable way, I also felt that I had let myself and everybody else down.

Happily, for reasons I will now explain, this state of affairs was not destined to last long.

Not very long after my inconclusive, even negative encounter with the word *Vedanta*, which was soon forgotten, I discovered one day, as I came into the house, that a hush had descended over it. We kids had been instructed that the main room was strictly out of bounds, but I did manage to sneak a look as I hurried away. On the large flat hard bed, my mother was lying prone, and my father was sitting solicitously nearby with what seemed like honey in his hand. There was no sense of crisis, but there was a certain gravity in the air.

When life returned to normal, which was soon, we discovered that my mother had felt faint to the point of almost collapsing and feared that she had had a heart attack. And the freeze-frame in my memory was of our father giving her honey to drink as an immediate reaction to her feeling faint and drained. Upon further medical examination, it turned out to be a false alarm. The problem lay not with the heart but with a nerve close to it, and was easily remedied.

But the incident apparently put the fear of God in my mother. This nervous ailment may have only mimicked a heart attack, but it served as an intimation of mortality for my mother.

Not long after this incident, my parents heard of a series of lectures on Advaita Vedanta, which were to be delivered by one Swami Chinmayananda. Often upon returning from school, we children would find them headed for the lectures. We too were invited to attend but only if we felt like going.

I started attending these lectures on a fairly regular basis. I am still not quite certain why. I must have been thirteen around this time. I had dabbled a bit in yoga around this time—in the form of *japa* (repeating a verbal formula thousands of time to produce its effect). I had annoyed my sisters by trying to hypnotize them and tried to contact the spirits—who had told the group which did this, on a regular basis, that my satchel at school had been stolen by the school servant. But this was serious intellectual stuff. I heard such words as *Brahma, Ātmā, Upaniṣad* for the first time.

I was not even curious about the Swami in the ochre robe, who taught the classes. I had seen so many of them. He used to address a reasonably large crowd. If one arrived in the time, one was expected to chant the following invocation:

Invocation

> *Sa ha nāv avatu, saha nau bhunaktu, saha vīryaṁ karavāvahai; tejasvi nav adhītam astu: mā vidviṣāvahai; aum śāntiḥ śāntiḥ, śāntiḥ*
>
> May He protect us both; may He be pleased with us both; may we work together with vigour; may our study make us illuminated; may there be no dislike between us. *Aum*, peace, peace, peace.[1]

I have no idea how much I grasped of what I heard. But I do not ever remember feeling bored.

Soon, however, school work took precedence. Then, my father was transferred to a place called Rewa in Madhya Pradesh. I enrolled at the college there, and I remember Swami Chinmayananda coming down there and delivering some lectures. These lectures were on the *Kena Upanishad*. At the end, he announced a prize for a fifty-page essay on the *Kena Upanishad*. I took up the challenge.

Then, my father was posted to Allahabad, and by now, I was pursuing my baccalaureate. There too, Swami Chinmayananda came and delivered a series of lectures. The energetic pursuit of my academic studies prevented me from attending them. He would, however, sometimes also give private audiences. I found the time to attend some of these. Some of what I heard during these audiences left a mark on my memory.

One memory I have is of an explanation of the Swami's frequent use of snuff, which was supposed to keep an intestinal ailment of his in check. We had wondered how the Swami might have contracted this ailment. Then, one day we found out. After his initiation into *sannyasa*—while receiving instruction from his own guru, Tapovana Maharaja, who also hailed from Kerala—the Swami would roam in the Himalayas. It so happened that, one day in the course of these wandering, he ran into bad weather and took shelter in a cave to avoid the perils of the storm. He had not been long in the cave when he discovered that he had a companion in the form of a bear, who occupied another nook of the cave, also presumably hoping to sit out the storm. Upon realizing the presence of the bear, the Swami said, "a sense of fear entered my mind." This bothered him greatly because when one becomes a renunciant one is supposed to renounce everything—including fear. The fact that he felt fear was a reproach for him as a *sannyasi* (renunciant). So, in order to remain true to his calling, he resolved, come what may, to spend the rest of the night right there in the company of the very bear—whose presence had struck him with fear.

The day dawned, and man and beast went their separate ways. But the price of the attainment of mental fearlessness was a physical ailment. On account of the exposure to the cold, the Swami developed acute diarrhea, so acute that he could barely walk two paces without having to relieve himself. His intestinal ailment was the legacy of that death-defying night.

Another account also involved his roamings in the Himalayas. He had heard of a great Master and desired an interview with him. He was able to reach the Master, and the interview went well, although Swami Chinmayananda sensed some traces of physical discomfort in his interlocutor but not such as to cause concern. When it was time to leave the Master, whom Swamiji was visiting, the Master begged to be excused from not following the courtesy of walking the visitor to the door. It was then that Swami Chinmayananda noted a ghastly sight: his host's entire foot was infested with worms.

Swamiji was shocked beyond measure, but the Master explained, "I am an old man. I do not have much longer to live. These worms have arrived a little ahead of time. It behooves us to be hospitable."

I had heard that hospitality is a prized virtue in Hinduism, but I had not expected to see it carried to such lengths.

It was also at these sittings that Swami Chinmayananda recounted an encounter with his own guru, Tapovanaji Maharaja, whose pedagogical value will not be lost on students of Advaita Vedanta.

It is a fundamental premise of Advaita Vedanta that the ultimate reality may be described, to the extent that it is amenable to description in words, as *nirguṇa brahman* or as an ultimate reality (*brahman*), which is devoid of any distinguishing characteristics, (but this does not mean that it is characterless). The same reality was also described as *saguṇa brahman* in relation to the universe, when it possesses the characteristic, for instance, of sustaining it. But, as this is in relation to the world which is ultimately unreal, the relationship of the universe to the *brahman* is also ultimately unreal; therefore, *saguna brahman* is also unreal, although both *nirguṇa* and *saguṇa* are two aspects of *brahman*.

Swami Chinmayananda insisted, in his discussion with his guru, on the dispensability of the term *saguṇa brahman* in that case: why entertain it as a category if it is ultimately unreal in relation to *brahman*, the only ultimately real? The whole morning was taken up in this animated debate, and Swamiji's guru could not bring Swamiji to see his point.

Finally, the guru said, "Let us have a break, and then we will resume the discussion. In the meantime, could you please fetch me some water."

Swami Chinmayananda dutifully rose, fetched a glass of water, and handed over that glass of water to his guru.

At this, the guru lost his temper. The guru went wild with rage. He shouted at Swami Chinmayananda, "You mutt. I had asked you for *water*; why have you given me a *glass*."

And the dumbstruck Swami Chinmayananda, not used to such Zen-like display of temper by his guru, stood there dumbfounded muttering,: "glass . . . water . . . water . . . glass."

The moral of the story is obvious to anyone who has struggled with *nirguṇa brahman* and *saguṇa brahman* as constituting two aspects of the same reality but there are two other morals hidden in there, which might be less obvious. It, of course, has to do with the much talked about master-disciple (*guru-sisya*) relation within Hinduism. This incident puts the finger on its essence—that the guru assumes *personal responsibility* for making the disciple see the light.

> A story from the Puranas about Sage Ribhu and his disciple Nidagha is particularly instructive in this context. Although Ribhu taught his disciple the supreme Truth of the One Brahman without a second, Nidagha, in spite of his erudition and understanding, did not get sufficient conviction to adopt and follow the path of *jnana*, but settled down in his native town to lead a life devoted to the observance of ceremonial religion.
>
> But the Sage loved his discipline as deeply as the latter venerated his Master. In spite of his age, Ribhu would himself go to his disciple in the town, just to see how far the latter had outgrown his ritualism. At times the Sage went in disguise, so that he might observe how Nidagha would act when he did not know that he was being observed by his Master.
>
> On one such occasion Ribhu, who had put on the disguise of a village rustic, found Nidagha intently watching a royal procession. Unrecognized by the town-dweller Nidagha, the village rustic inquired that the bustle was all about, and was told that the king was going in procession.

"Oh! It is the king. He goes in procession! But where is he?" asked the rustic.

"There, on the elephant," said Nidagha.

"You say the king is on the elephant. Yes, I see the two," said the rustic. "But which is the king and which is the elephant?"

"What!" exclaimed Nidagha. "You see the two, but do not know that the man above is the king and the animal below is the elephant? What is the use of talking to a man like you?"

"Pray, be not impatient with an ignorant man like me," begged the rustic. "But you said 'above' and 'below'—what do they mean?"

Nidagha could stand it no more. "You see the king and the elephant, the one *above* and the other *below*. Yet you want to know what is meant by 'above' and 'below'?" burst out Nidagha. "If things seen and words spoken can convey so little to you, action alone can teach you. Bend forward and you will know it all too well."

The rustic did as he was told. Nidagha got on his shoulders and said, "Know it now. I am *above* as the king; you are *below* as the elephant. Is that clear enough?"

"No, not yet," was the rustic's quiet reply. "You say you are above like the king and I am below like the elephant. The 'king,' the 'elephant,' 'above,' and 'below,' so far it is clear. But pray, tell me what you mean by '*I* ' and '*you*'?"

When Nidagha was thus confronted all of a sudden with the mighty problem of defining the "you" apart from the "I," light dawned on his mind. At once he jumped down and fell at his Master's feet, saying, "Who else but my venerable Master, Ribhu, could have thus drawn my mind from the superficialities of physical existence to the true Being of Self? O benign Master, I crave the blessings."[2]

The story has another moral: beware of Hindu gods and gurus asking you to fetch a glass of water!

Through prolonged austerities and devotional practices, Narada had won the grace of Vishnu. The god had appeared before the saint in his hermitage and granted him the fulfillment of a wish. "Show me the magic power of your Maya," Narada had prayed, and the god had replied, "I will. Come with me"; but again with that ambiguous smile on his beautifully curved lips.

From the pleasant shadow of the sheltering hermit grove, Vishnu conducted Narada across a bare stretch of land which blazed like metal under the merciless glow of a scorching sun. The two were soon very thirsty. At some distance, in the glaring light, they perceived the thatched roofs of a tiny hamlet. Vishnu asked: "Will you go over there and *fetch me some water*?"

"Certainly, O Lord," the saint replied, and he made off to the distant group of huts. The god relaxed under the shadow of a cliff, to await his return.

When Narada reached the hamlet, he knocked at the first door. A beautiful maiden opened to him and the holy man experienced something of which he had never up to that time dreamed: the enchantment of her eyes. They resembled those of his divine Lord and friend. He stood and gazed. He simply forgot what he had come for. The girl, gentle and candid, bade him welcome. Her voice was a golden noose about his neck. As though moving in a vision, he entered the door.

The occupants of the house were full of respect for him, yet not the least bit shy. He was honorably received, as a holy man, yet somehow not as a stranger; rather, as an old and venerable acquaintance who had been a long time away. Narada remained with them impressed by their cheerful and noble bearing, and feeling entirely at home. Nobody asked him what he had come for; he seemed to have belonged to the family from time immemorial. And after a certain period, he asked the father for permission to marry the girl, which was no more than everyone in the house had been expecting. He became a member of the family and shared with them the age-old burdens and simple delights of a peasant household.

Twelve years passed; he had three children. When his father-in-law died he became head of the household, inheriting the estate and managing it, tending the cattle and cultivating the fields. The twelfth year, the rainy season was extraordinarily violent: the streams swelled, torrents poured down the hills, and the little village was inundated by a sudden flood. In the night, the straw huts and cattle were carried away and everybody fled.

With one hand supporting his wife, with the other leading two of his children, and bearing the smallest on his shoulder, Narada set forth hastily. Forging ahead through the pitch darkness and lashed by the rain, he waded through slippery mud, staggered through whirling waters. The burden was more than he could manage with the current heavily dragging at his legs. Once, when he stumbled, the child slipped from his shoulder and disappeared in the roaring night. With a desperate cry, Narada let go the older children to catch at the smallest, but was too late.

Meanwhile, the flood swiftly carried off the other two, and even before he could realize the disaster, ripped from his side his wife, swept his own feet from under him and flung him headlong in the torrent like a log. Unconscious, Narada was stranded eventually on a little cliff. When he returned to consciousness, he opened his eyes upon a vast sheet of muddy water. He could only weep.

"Child!" He heard a familiar voice, which nearly stopped his heart. "Where is the water you went to fetch for me? I have been waiting more than half an hour."[3]

II

I also entered the Hindu world through some unexpected portals.

According to tradition, one is supposed to learn about one's religion from one's father. But my father was more into the poet Wordsworth than into Hinduism. And I discovered the meaning of the Wordsworthian dictum—the child is the father of man—the wrong way. Through a family oversight, I ended up with Sanskrit as one of my subjects, and when my father would quote some British author he was reading in English about some aspect of Hinduism, I would usually demolish his point by citing a Sanskrit verse to the contrary. There was more than one such occasion, but one I remember vividly. He quoted someone called Mackenzie to the effect that Hindus have no ethics.[4]

"What is ethics?" I asked.

"O, caring for the welfare of others," my father said in an offhand way.

"And Hinduism lacks it?"[5] I wondered aloud. "But then why do we end our prayers with the chant:

> May all be at ease;
> May all be sinless;
> May all experience happiness;
> May none experience suffering.[6]

He knew enough Hindi to follow the simple Sanskrit of the verse, and upon hearing it, my father fell silent. However, later when I began studying Wordsworth in my English class, I exchanged my somewhat egotistical understanding of the child being the father of the man to a better one.

But now, I realize that, in a way, my father did instruct me in Hinduism. Wordsworth was his favorite poet—though when he once described him as the "greatest poet in the world," I put it down to his anglomania. I was only awakening intellectually to the doctrine of rebirth in Hinduism when I heard him recite one day:

> Our birth is but a sleep and a forgetting;
> The soul that rises with us, our life's star,
> Hath had elsewhere its setting,
> And cometh from afar;
> Not in entire forgetfulness,
> And not in utter nakedness,
> But trailing clouds of glory do we come
> From God, who is our home.[7]

So, perhaps in his own way, he did instruct me in Hinduism—Wordsworthily, that is. Once, when we were planning to visit an *ashram* (hermitage), he said, "That is good" and then went on:

> The world is too much with us; late and soon,
> Getting and spending, we lay waste our powers;
> Little we see in Nature that is ours:
> We have given our hearts away, a sordid boon!
> This sea that bares her bosom to the moon,
> The winds that will be howling at all hours,
> And are up-gathered now like sleeping flowers.
> For this for, everything, we are out of tune.[8]

My father and I perhaps embody a generational change in our attitude toward British rule, but the divergence seems to be less marked when it comes to English literature. Rudyard Kipling, for instance, has a reputation, among Indians at least, of being an imperialist author. Yet, after reading the following poem by him, I can't stop wondering whether he was familiar with the *Bhagavadgītā* (famously translated into English in 1785 by Charles Wilkins and then in 1885 by Edwin Arnold, with numerous other translations):

If

If you can keep your head when all about you
Are losing theirs and blaming it on you,
If you can trust yourself when all men doubt you,
But make allowance for their doubting too;
If you can wait and not be tired by waiting,
Or being lied about, don't deal in lies,
Or being hated, don't give way to hating,
And yet don't look too good, nor talk too wise:
If you can dream—and not make dreams your master;
If you can think—and not make thought your aim;
If you can meet with Triumph and Disaster
And treat those two imposters just the same;
If you can bear to hear the truth you've spoken
Twisted by knaves to make a trap for fools,
Or watch the things you gave your life to, broken,
And stoop and build 'em up with worn-out tools:

If you can make one heap of all your winnings
And risk it on one turn of pitch-and-toss,
And lose, and start again at your beginnings
And never breathe a word about your loss;
If you can force your heart and nerve and sinew
To serve your turn long after they are gone,
And so hold on when there is nothing in you
Except the will which says to them: "Hold on!"

If you can talk with crowds and keep your virtue,
Or walk with kings—nor lose the common touch,
If neither foes nor loving friends can hurt you,
If all men count with you, but none too much;
If you can fill the unforgiving minute
With sixty seconds' worth of distance run,
Yours is the Earth and everything that's in it,
And—which is more—you'll be a Man, my son!

When I read it I clipped and attached the poem to my copy of the *Bhagavadgītā*. I think it is its best rendering in English.

Or perhaps, the essence of the *Bhagavadgītā* is also contained in the following verses found on the desk of Pandit Nehru, India's first prime minister, when he passed away in May 1964.

> The woods are lovely, dark and deep
> But I have promises to keep
> And miles to go before I sleep
> And miles to go before I sleep.[9]

PART II

The Hinjew Connection

Are Hindus born with a Jewish gene? How else to explain the Hinjew connection, the soft spot Hindus, by and large, have for the Jews?

Even while reading Shakespeare in school I felt uneasy about the depiction of Shylock, salivating for his pound of flesh. Something was wrong here. I could never quite put my finger on it. I registered the word *anti-Semitism* for the first time only when in the States.

It seems to me sometimes that anti-Hinduism in the Western media and academia is as virulent as anti-Semitism, without receiving the benefit of a similar recognition and critique. That's another story, but it needs to be told some day, for anti-Semitism and anti-Hinduism, as morphological acts of aggression, bear a resemblance.

The diary of Anne Frank, as soon as it was published, caught my attention, as soon as it began being proclained about. Part of my juvenile poetic efforts consisted of a sonnet dedicated to her when I was eighteen. I can still recall the first line, though vaguely: "If only we were few but firm as Jew." Mercifully, I don't remember the rest of the sonnet! But it is the thought that counts, and what thoughts could count for more than the following thoughts of Mahadev Govind Ranade (1842–1901), one of the lights of the so-called Hindu renaissance. This is what he said in 1893 in Lahore (now in Pakistan):

> If the miraculous preservation of a few thousand Jews had a purpose, this more miraculous preservation of one-fifth of the human race is not due to mere chance.[1]

Later, in a speech delivered in Calcutta in 1896, he even couched the aspirations of this one-fifth of humanity in the idiom of the promised land.

> With a liberated manhood, with buoyant hope, with a faith that never shirks duty, with a sense of justice that deals fairly to all, with unclouded intellect and powers fully cultivated, and lastly, with a love that overleaps all bounds, renovated India will take her proper rank among the nations of the world, and be the master of the situation and of her own destiny. This is the goal to be reached—*this is the promised land.*[2]

The promised land! How the Jews longed for Zion during the Babylonian Exile:

> By the rivers of Babylon,
> There we sat down, and wept,
> When we remembered Zion.
> Upon the poplars. In the midst of her,
> We hung up our harps.
> For there our captors
> Demanded of us songs,
> And our tormentors, mirth:
> "Sing us some of the songs of Zion."
>
> How could we sing the songs of the Lord
> In a foreign land?
> If I forget you, O Jerusalem,
> May my right hand fail me!
> May my tongue cleave to my palate,
> If I do not remember you;
> If I set not Jerusalem above my highest joy![3]

Now, the Hindu longs for the achievements of the Jewish state, the way the Jews longed for Zion. First, in the wilderness for forty years and them almost for thousand—but the Jews got there. The Hindu has been in exile in his own land for a thousand years, and in his more anguished moments even now, like the Son of Man, knows not where to rest his head.

I think what draws Judaism and Hinduism together is their shared status as ethnic religions and their shared perception that they have both been at the receiving ends of the Islamic and Christian missionary sticks, as they spurned these carrots of conversion. Does common bondage explain common binding—even though explanation is historical rather than genetic? The genetic is too farfetched anyway, although marriages between Hindus and Jews are not unknown.

The historical experience of the Hindus and the Jews provides a parallel. When I first read about the rise of Rabbinic Judaism after the destruction of the Temple by the Romans, I remember being tremendously impressed by the intelligent quality of the Jewish response in the midst of what must have been such an emotional situation, in which one would have expected emotion to override reason. However, the Jewish leaders correctly assessed the futility of a martial response to the Roman challenge. Indeed, they perhaps saw in it an invitation to annihilation and, instead, proceeded to wrap the tradition in the protective cocoon of law. How successful they were in this strategy, not only in the short-term but also over the long haul, may be gauged from the fact that the Jewish community not only survived its confrontation with Christianity but also went on to survive its confrontation with Islam. On this latter point, Christianity actually suffered by comparison, because it was virtually wiped out in the areas conquered by the Muslims, while Jewish communities averted such a fate, and, unlike the Christian community, continued to flourish during Islamic rule.

It was only later I learnt that the strategy Hindu thinkers adopted in the face of the challenge posed by Islam to them bears a striking similarity to the one adopted by Jewish thinkers in the face of the Roman onslaught.

> The service which a small priestly class rendered to a whole people at the time of the destruction of [Hindu] political power is paralleled only by the action of the Jewish rabbis when the Temple was destroyed and Jews dispersed by the Romans. At the time when the Jewish people sank into despair, a group of learned men under Johanan ben Zakkai established the great academy at Jabneh in the heart of Roman Palestine itself and guarded zealously the doctrine of Judaism. It sent its messages to the Jewish people dispersed all over the world and thus saved Judaism for the future. That is what the Brahmins did in the 13th and the 14th centuries in the Gangetic Valley.[4]

The parallel is fascinating because of both, its similarity and difference. Apart from the obvious historical similarity, I think the two religions—Hinduism and Judaism—heighten our appreciation of the fact that the followers of a religious tradition are not just participants in the tradition but also makers of it. They do not merely receive a tradition but also modify it as they pass it along. They don't merely ape it but also shape it—a fact which often gets overlooked. As for the difference: In the case of Judaism, with its transformation into Rabbinic Judaism, the leadership of the community passed from the hands of a hereditary priesthood into that of a meritocratic self-recruited rabbinate, based not on birth but education, for which any male could qualify. This did not quite happen that way in Hinduism, although the way the poet-saints of medieval Hinduism and the reformers of modern Hinduism shaped the tradition does seem to indicate that the leadership of the community did not remain confined to the hands of a hereditary priesthood.

So, a subtle difference surfaces here between Judaism and Hinduism. In Judaism, the rabbis replaced the Levis; in Hinduism, the saints and swamis, who unlike the priests, renounce the world, supplemented the priesthood. Both traditions held their ground.

But there is another difference. India has always been ahead in the numbers game. Even Herodotus records that Indians were by far the largest in number among all the peoples known to him. And if current trends hold, India is set to wrest this dubious distinction from China in 2025. But I digress. The point is that, although both Hindus and Jews have survived, the Hindus were so numerous and the Jews so few! But it does not mean that the Hindus did not have their own version of the Holocaust. Although swamis do not make the best statisticians, let us hear what Swami Vivekananda has to say:

> When the Mohammedans first came, we are [told] I think on the authority of Ferishta, the oldest Mohammedan historian—to have been six hundred million Hindus. Now [in 1899] we are about two hundred million.[5]

A Hindu holocaust? If the word *holocaust* means a burnt offering then let it be remembered the Hindus burn the dead. If the Jewish Holocaust decimated a third of European Jewry, do we not have a similar phenomenon here—only on a grander scale? Or does the scalar (as distinguished from a proportionate) shift alter the phenomenon, and a change in quantity leads to a change in quality (a point Marxists love to make).

Let us set these gruesome nuances aside—a civilizational version of Sophie's choice. Let us address the issue of the Holocaust itself.

There are numerous books on the philosophy of religion, which regularly include a chapter on theodicy. There are also numerous books on the Holocaust. But in the chapters on theodicy, in the books on the philosophy of religion, there is hardly any mention of the Holocaust! It seems to me that the Holocaust raises a fundamental question in relation to theodicy for the philosophers of religion: namely, how, is such a phenomenon to be reconciled with God's providence?

Irrespective of whether the problem is compounded or not by the fact of more than one holocaust, if such is the case, the problem is still rendered more intractable by the Jewish case. "Why?" you ask. And that stops me cold in the tracks, but only temporarily. I grant you the question: Why rent yourselves bald over six million deaths in the Holocaust, when the Second World War itself claimed fifty million lives? Does not the loss of fifty million lives pose a greater challenge for a theodicy than the loss of six million?

The point has its force but the case of a holocaust, it seems to me, does introduce a new element in the situation. The collateral damage of any war, no matter how massive, is itself not "targeted," although it results from firing on targets. In a holocaust the group itself is the target, so the question moves from the sphere on evil in general to that of particularized evil. The following account from the narratives of the life of Guru Nanak (1469–1539) may help us in drawing this distinction:

> One day Mardānā asked, "Why have so many been slain when only one did wrong?"
>
> "Go and sleep under that tree, Mardānā," answered the Guru. "When you get up I shall give you an answer."
>
> And so Mardānā went and slept there. Now a drop of grease had fallen on his chest while he was eating and while he was sleeping it attracted ants.
>
> One ant happened to disturb the sleeping Mardānā who responded by wiping them all away with his hand.
>
> "What have you done, Mardānā?" asked Bābā Nānak.
>
> "All have died because one disturbed me," exclaimed Mardānā.
>
> Bābā Nānak laughed and said, "Mardānā, thus does death come to many because of one."[6]

This provides an illustration of heavy collateral damage. But the expression, "Thus does death come to many because of one," can be taken in two senses. The *one* here could either be the one ant who disturbed Mardānā, or it could be the *one* Mardānā, if he had consciously set out to destroy all the ants.

Most of theodicy seems to proceed without making this key distinction. Once the distinction is made, it becomes clear that there are two types of cases involved and that one constitutes a graver moral issue than the other, for it raises the question: "Why me?" to the level of "Why us?"—or why "He or him" to that of "Why them?."

In Guru Nanak's own time, India witnessed the invasion of Babur (d. 1530), and Nanak himself bears testimony to the tragic loss of life it involved. In his words that follow, Yama represents the Hindu god of death:

> Thou, O creator of all things,
> Takest to thyself no blame.
> Thou hast sent Yama disguised as the great Moghal,
> Babar.
> Terrible was the slaughter,
> Loud were the cries of the lamenters.
> Did this not awaken pity in Thee, O Lord?
> Thou art part and parcel of all things equally, O Creator:
> Thou must feel for all men and all nations.
> If a strong man attacketh who is equally strong,
> Where is the grief in this, or whose is the grievance?
> But when a fierce tiger preys on the helpless cattle,
> The Herdsman must answer for it.[7]

Guru Nanak could have invoked the readymade doctrine of karma to come to terms with the tragedy, which then would amount to neither blaming Mardānā nor one ant, but each ant for its own death!

But back to Mardānā. Mardānā did not set out to destroy all ants, nor Babar to kill only Hindus. The major king he defeated was a Muslim, but Hitler apparently set out to destroy all European Jews. It might be invidious to distinguish one evil from another as all are tarred with the same brush. I think we will be inclined to admit that one which involves a defined group of people specifically is of a darker hue. It makes up in its singularity what it loses in its scope. Why would anyone want to do that?

The numerous Jewish followers of the Hindu god-man Sai Baba must have felt tormented by the same question. One of them, it is said, did ask him about the Holocaust. And he is believed to have said, "There is no effect without a cause." The answer is suitably laconic in terms of guruspeak, but it is also cryptic. What complicates the issue for us is the further fact that the famous woman saint of modern India, Anandmayee Ma (whose devotees included Mrs. Indira Gandhi) is believed to have offered the same unsolicited remark, on her own, at the height of the Hindu-Muslim riots, around the time of India's independence. And this was one of the few occasions when she permitted herself a comment on public events! Does her comment help us or hinder us? What is the parallel here? That just as Hitler was trying to exterminate the Jews, the Hindus and Muslims was trying to exterminate each other—or without yielding to any further subtleties, is there no parallel here other than a reference to large scale slaughter?

"Why the Holocaust," I asked a Jewish friend as we sat in the cafeteria between classes.

"I don't know," she said, "But, when I came to this school, my Christian friends wondered why I had not converted to Christianity—even after the Holocaust and all, you know."

I was puzzled, "Why should they expect you to convert to Christianity on account of the Holocaust?"

"It constituted an empirical confirmation of the fact that the Jews were a cursed race on account of having killed Jesus. They call it deicide—killing God," she continued.

"What they said to you about the Holocaust seems to me to contain an explanation of the Holocaust and to that extent I am less bewildered." But then I leaned forward and asked,: "On two points I am more bewildered. Was Jesus God? And can God be killed?"

I admit I am from India, but she looked at me as if I was from another planet. And I felt as if I was from another planet. Then she said, "Anything is possible in Christianity," her despair turning into sarcasm, although it was not clear to me whether she had despaired of me or Christianity.

"Anything is possible in Hinduism, too," I responded. "But those who are killed are revived in its realm of infinite possibilities."

And talking of Rabbinic Judaism . . .

There are some lines which lodge themselves in one's consciousness forever the moment one reads them for the first time. For me, the following line of Hillel is one such line:

> If I am not for myself, who will be for me? And being for myself, who am I? And if not now, when?

The excruciatingly exquisite way in which the first two lines adjust the rival claims of individualism and altruism, of self-regarding and other-regarding ethics is unsurpassed, and may be unsurpassable. But, as soon as I came under its spell, as a human being, it was almost broken by my awareness as a comparative religionist: is this the way the tradition itself understands it? I could remember my disillusionment when I discovered, as a historian of religion, that turning the other cheek, or returning evil with good, did not quite have the same meaning for early Christians as I had taken it to mean. I had taken it as a great moral statement, a statement in line with the following lines so dear to Mahatma Gandhi, who had also rephrased the Christian injunction in its sublimest sense:

> For a bowl of water give a goodly meal;
> For a kindly greeting bow down with zeal;
> For a simple penny pay thou back with gold;
> If thy life be rescued, life do not withold.
> Thus the words and actions of the wise regard;
> Every little service tenfold they reward.
> But the truly noble know all men as one,
> And return with gladness good for evil done.[8]

The emphasis in all along on returning good with greater good, until the last three lines turn the tables and deepen the dialectic, aligning it with the Christian—of returning even evil with good.

I learnt in the New Testament class that, when taken in its context, the exhortation to resist no evil was an eschatological statement, not so much an ethical one. I was told what it really meant was that the Day of Judgment is around the corner—just around the corner, any day, even any moment—so why even bother with getting even, when God will be rendering justice any day now. As the professor said, "Why go about touting your toy guns, when the atomic blast is around the corner." That took the moral shine off it—at least for me, at least for some time.

So, I dreaded the day when I would discover what that epigrammatic utterance of Hillel means within Judaism itself. But how long can a comparative religionist hope to remain innocent about averting evil in such matters? The dreaded day arrived when I read the following lines with mounting exegetical excitement:

> We learn from Hillel in The Wisdom of the Fathers: "If I am not for myself, who will be for me? And being for myself, what am I? And if not now, when?" According to the Talmudic rabbis and rabbinic commentators, this compressed dialectic had to do with the individual accumulation of merit through adhering to the prescribed Jewish way of life; a person should acquire merit for himself and not

depend on others to perform good deeds on his behalf; and since he is under equal obligation to make others do good, he should also teach others the right way. But the Jewish folk came to understand Hillel's teaching corporately, as a political directive that they should not expect anyone else to stand up on their behalf unless they have first learned to stand up for themselves. Primo Levi, who survived almost a full year in Auschwitz, entitled his novel about a band of Jewish partisans, "If Not Now When," citing these words from a partisan song:

> Brothers away from this Europe of graves.
> Let us climb together towards the land
> Where we will be men among men.
> If I am not for myself, who will be for me?
> If not this way, how? If not now, when?

For the partisans, and for us, the words of Hillel became a Zionist imperative. Because the Jewish struggle for freedom is always launched against political despotism, it benefits everyone else who truly clings to freedom. But it follows from this imperative that if we Jews fail to stand up for ourselves we also fail the cause of freedom.[9]

My understanding, I discovered, fell between the classical and the modern one. I wonder at this point what the reader took Hillel to be saying, and how he or she resolves the dilemma of cherishing an utterance in a lofty meaning of one's own, which turns out to be at variance with its "original" meaning! Not that one needs to feel too crestfallen about it, for if the "Torah has seventy faces," should it include only the utterances of those who master it—the rabbis. Nevertheless, it is not a trifling matter for a comparative religionist's conscience, if, between his understanding and that of the tradition, there falls the shadow of discrepancy.

I was led to the book in which I located the Jewish understanding of Hillel's saying by its enticing title, *If I Am Not for Myself: The Liberal Betrayal of the Jews.* As I read more into it, however, my initial sense of discomfort dissolved, as I found my own experiences as a Hindu being reflected back to me as in a mirror through the experience of the Jews described in those pages. (There were certain passages after reading which I had to rub my eyes to be sure that I had read them right, and was not a victim of dyslexic self-deception.)

There were entire passages in this book, in some of which all you had to do was to change the word *Jew* to *Hindu* and the whole passage would then seamlessly apply in toto to the Hindu reality. The similarities were so uncanny that it led me to entertain the academically grotesque idea of plagiarizing the whole book! All I had to do was to replace the word *Jew* with *Hindu,* and I had a new book! When I shared with the author my audacious project of virtually hijacking her entire work in this manner, what kept me on the straight and narrow path was her gentle admonition that this was a practice generally discouraged in legitimate scholarship. OK, I got carried away. But if you think I am exaggerating, consider the following passages, in which all that I have done is to change the word *Jew* to *Hindu*:

> Distinguished from Christian and Muslims . . . *Hindus* have not attempted to win other peoples over to their vision of redemption and have thus avoided the temptations of political power. But being, as they were, at the mercy of other peoples, their corresponding temptation was making a virtue of powerlessness.[10]

> A people . . . at once so cosmopolitan in instincts and so tribal in their obligations, so politically vulnerable and so ultimately indissoluble.[11]

> *Hindu* "parochialism" is always implicitly universal, since *Hindu* law recognizes both the legitimate existence of other peoples and the right of everyone who genuinely desires it to become a *Hindu*. By contrast, universal idealism in religion and politics is always implicitly repressive, since it expects everyone to become its particular species of universalism.[12]

> As we have already suggested, the high ratio in *Hindu* civilization of self-blame over self-praise has always encouraged individual morality at the expense of political self-confidence.[13]

> The cultural assumptions of *Hindus* were often antithetical to those of their neighbours, so that they were prevented by both the nature and the angle of their cultural vision from knowing the hatred that consumed them. As a result, the art that *Hindus* produced about their own history is

> dramatically skewed, and the dramatic bias is always in danger of slipping into moral bias. Unable to dramatize the evildoers, yet intimately acquainted with both the manifold shortcomings of the *Hindu*, *Hindu* writers (and *Hindu* intellectuals) are always in danger of charging their fellow *Hindus* for incurring the hatred against them.[14]

> Since his will to innocence requires that he have no enemies, he must hold his fellow *Hindus* responsible for the enemies he has.[15]

> "I see through you," he said. "I see through you. You'd like not to have any enemies in life. Yes, that's what you keep trying to arrange for yourself—to have no enemies."[16]

Perhaps, it is only with the help of the Jewish experience that the world will understand what it meant for the Indians, mostly Hindus, to be able to say openly that "China is our potential enemy number one"—what it means for a people to be able to say this, who for a thousand years have kept trying to arrange for themselves not to have any enemies in life or death.

Experiencing Christianity

I

I had sought admission to the Harvard Divinity School in the pursuit of comparative religion. Once I had been there for a while I saw no reason to exclude Christianity from my purview. So, one Sunday I betook myself to a morning mass at church.

There were first the choir songs, then the reading from the Bible followed by the sermon—that is the staple of any service. I knew these to be the ingredients of a Christian service—though not necessarily in that order. I had picked up my ideas of what constitutes a Christian service piecemeal so I knew the pieces but not quite how they fit.

But nothing had prepared me for what was to follow—I mean the Eucharist. When I was told "this (the wine) is the blood of Jesus Christ" and "this (the wafer) is the flesh," I was ready to go into shock.

This was blatant and rampant cannibalism! I was quite horrified. At first, I put it down to a Hindu's distaste for nonvegetarianism. But no, this was way beyond that. This was cannibalism.

As I write this, the sense of recoiling horror begins to come back to me.

Why was I so shocked?

In trying to analyze my own reaction, I have come to grapple with many possibilities. But, before I soften or dilute my experience with explanations, let me first share with you once again the raw nature of my experience. When I read the following description of the Eucharist recently by Swami Dayananda, I found that it reflected my sense of religious outrage as well as anything I could say myself:

> Can a cultured man even do such a thing? Only an ignorant savage would do it. No enlightened man could ever call the food of his disciples his flesh nor their drink his blood . . . they eat and drink imagining all the time that their bread was the flesh of Christ and their drink his blood. Is this not an awful thing? How could those who could not keep aloof from the idea that their food and drink were the flesh and blood of their Saviour, abstain from the flesh and blood of others.[1]

Not my sentiments *exactly* but pretty close.

This is how I figure out why I may have reacted the way I did.

(1) I was brought up in a Hindu family, which more or less abjured the use of meat and wine. Not that nobody ate meat—some did, and I did too sometimes. But essentially we were vegetarians. In any case, vegetarianism was definitely an inherited value, and abstention from alcohol even more so. Imbibing was definitely higher up on the ladder of sin. To witness both of these violated right before my eyes in the *name of religion* was a bit too much to take.

(2) There is a form of Hinduism which does use wine and meat in its rituals, but it is the Tantric form of Hinduism and was considered quite degenerate in India (although this assessment is now undergoing modification). So, this is what Christianity was: a degenerate Tantric sect?

(3) I had formed the impression that, just as man qua human being stands at the crest of the evolutionary wave biologically, Christianity thought of itself in the same position religiously. But the rite I was observing seemed so savage and primitive as to defy description—even reaction. So, here was Christianity in its true colors! It was really at the bottom of the totem pole and not the top. Basically, the emperor had no clothes, despite all the verbal rhetorical vestments Christian evangelists use to cover it up.

My explosive reaction was perhaps the outcome of a combustible combination of my Hindu background and Christian conceit. And, then suddenly, a bulb lit up; it dawned on me: this is how Hindu customs must have appeared to its Christian observers. No wonder we get such distorted accounts of Hinduism from Western sources.

This self-reflection pacified me somewhat. Then, I asked myself a basic question I have trained myself to ask when I encounter some indigestible element in another tradition: do you think these people are fools to continue to practice this ritual in such large numbers for centuries?

I grant that this approach may not work with *cognitive* facts. Apparently millions of people could continue believing for thousands of years that the earth was flat, or that the sun went round the earth. However, with *cultural* facts, I have found it useful to encourage myself to ask this question.

So I went home and read through the entire New Testament. And since then, I have never had any difficulty in attending, or in participating in the Eucharist.

Text—in this case a ritual text—without context is an invitation to alienation. I can testify to that.

II

I was basically doing nothing when an Indian fellow-student asked me as the class dispersed, "What are you doing now?"

"Nothing."

"Why don't you come to a lecture by Professor Stendahl on early Christianity?"

"Are you taking the course for credit?"

"No."

"Should I be taking it?"

"Are you?"

"No."

"Then?"

He didn't say it, but I think he thought the trouble with me was that I asked too many questions. Finally, he just said with admirable brevity, "Come. Just come."

I went. And went, and went.

I found there were many like me—who just sat in on the course to hear Professor Krister Stendahl lecture!

I shall never forget the last class before Christmas; not for the lecture (they were always memorable) but what happened after the lecture. As soon as he had finished speaking, the students in the front row started clapping. From there, it spread to the upper rows until the whole room was clapping. Then some students in the front row stood up still clapping. Soon, the students in the upper row were standing too—and then the whole hall stood up—still clapping.

While the clapping kept gently rising in volume, I could observe Prof. Stendahl gradually fold his papers, collect whatever material he had, and turn gradually toward the door that let him out. As he approached the door, the clapping rose to a crescendo. Prof. Stendahl's back was toward us as he approached the exit. Upon reaching it he paused, turned around, and raised his hand. The class went suddenly quiet. Then he smiled and said, "Merry Christmas." The class erupted in a mighty roar which swept the hall. And he was gone.

So, I said to myself, respect for teachers is not something unique to India. One could have wondered, seeing the way the students sometimes talk to the professors in America.

It was, thus, by living and learning in a Christian environment that I learnt to appreciate Christianity on its own terms. But my initial experience remains a painful, if salutary, reminder of how crossing over to another religion or culture may not be that easy. Why—a paranoid hyper-Hindu government could even ban the Eucharist as an unholy practice!

III

There are some things in religion which are hard to understand, perhaps because there is more to religion than logic—as there is to life, to which it is perhaps closer than to logic. One of these is the curious resolve of pious childless couples to sacrifice the firstborn to the very God whose gift it is! Why gain a child through prayer to lose it through sacrifice? Is there some dark hope at the heart of it all that once God has set the reproductive machinery in motion, he will neglect to stop it after the first taking, and others will follow? Or should one be more charitable and suggest that it is just a good story line?

For whatever reason, couples in lands as far apart as Canaan and India have struck such bargains with God. The one from Canaan is better known in the West, where Abraham and Isaac are better known, than their Vedic counterparts, who will enter the stage later.

These thoughts flooded my mind after the Remembrance Day on November 11, 1991 at the McGill University Chapel where I had found myself on the stage, along with my Christian colleagues, to observe the occasion, even reading out a biblical passage selected beforehand. The solemn moment was made more so, when the following poem by Wilfred Owen was also read out, seamlessly woven into the service:

> So Abram rose, and clave the wood, and went,
> And took the fire with him, and a knife.
> And as they sojourned both of them together,

Isaac the first-born spake and said, My Father,
Behold the preparations, fire and iron,
But where the lamb for this burn-offering?
The Abram bound the youth with belts and straps,
And builded parapets and trenches there,
And stretched forth the knife to slay his son,
When lo, an angel called him out of heaven,
Saying, lay not thy hand upon the lad,
Neither do anything to him. Behold
A ram, caught in a thicket by its horns;
Offer the Ram of pride instead of him.
But the old man would not so, but slew his son,—
And half the seed of Europe, one by one.[2]

Whether the idea of sacrificing the firstborn originated as a riveting story line, we do not know, but it becomes a fitting image, with a twist, of the horrors of war—specially of the first World War, even if made horribly beautiful by the fact that the body of one dead young officer yielded the following line of Tagore:

When I go from hence then let this be my parting word
That what I have seen is unsurpassable.[3]

I do wonder if ages to come shall look back on our nationalistic wars the way we look back at the ritual of human sacrifice. But I regress.

In the Hindu version of the story, the childless royal couple pray to Varuṇa (whom some identify with the Greek Ouranos "though phonetic difficulties make the identification uncertain"[4]) rather than to Yahweh but get the same result—a son, who was prayed for in a manner similar to Isaac. But, when the god comes demanding what he gave them, they tarry and buy time. Their son gets wind of the bizarre arrangement and, less obedient or more fearful than Isaac, takes off, and the father is then afflicted by an angry Varuṇa with dropsy. Finally, a sacrificial substitution is arranged, but it is not a ram, as in the Abrahamic account, but another child; so it is going to be someone else's son instead of one's own. This substituted son, however, has been wisely coached by a sage for the occasion. When about to be slain in sacrifice, he recites a hymn in praise of Varuṇa, who is so pleased to hear the hymn that the lad, Śunaḥṣepa by name, is unshackled. This incident is apparently alluded to in the following lines of the *ṚgVeda* (1. 24. 12–15)

12. By night, by day they tell me, as tells me too
This longing of my heart: "Whom Sunahsepa
Called upon, bound [and captive as he was],
Varuna, the king, may he release (*muc-*) us!"
13. For Sunahsepa, captive, manacled
To three stakes called upon the son of Aditi,
Varuna, the king, that he might free him:
May the wise one, undeceived, all fetters loose!
14. With obeisance, sacrifice, oblations we
Would pray away thine anger, Varuna:
Wise sovereign (*asura*), king, make loose our sins—
For thou hast power,—[the sins] we have incurred.
15. Make loose our fetters,—[loose] the uppermost,
[Loose] the nethermost, and [loose] the midmost:
Then, son Aditi, [firm] in thy covenant (*vrata*)
Will we sinless stand before [thy mother] Aditi![5]

What is the message here—flattery will get you anywhere, or forgiveness will get you anything? This is a point to ponder later as we move on with the story. With the king restored to Varuṇa's favor, then freed of his gruesome obligation and united with *his* own child, the question arose: who is now Śunaḥṣepa's father? (A question worthy of a Solomonic decision.) There were three candidates—his biological father (who sold him), the commercial father (who bought him), and the celestial father—Varuṇa (who freed him). All three paternities—biological, commercial, or celestial—were not held to be valid on the following grounds. The biological father lost his claim when he sold the son; the commercial father lost his claim the moment he allowed the son to be sacrificed, and God cannot claim the child because forgiving is God's profession. So, the sage who taught the child the prayer he recited in praise of Varuṇa was declared to be the true father.[6]

This meditation on paternity serves to take us back to Wilfred Owen's poem. The father slays the son in the poem, departing from the biblical narrative—and so do millions of fathers who allow their sons to go to war, departing even further from the message of the Bible, if it be understood as one for peace over war. And if a new paternity is sought here, will it lead to Christ's and Gandhi's? And Martin Luther King's?

It is by these steps that the somber remembrance of war was converted into a meditation on war (a meditation to be resumed once one has read the finest war poem arising from World War I):

In Flanders fields the poppies blow
Between the crosses row on row,
That mark our place; and in the sky
The larks, still bravely singing, fly
Scarce heard amidst the guns below.

We are the Dead. Short days ago
We lived, felt dawn, saw sunset glow,
Loved and were loved, and now we lie
In Flanders fields.

Take up our quarrel with the foe:
To you from failing hands we throw
The torch; be yours to hold it high.
If ye break faith with us who die
We shall not sleep, though poppies grow
In Flanders fields.[7]

The poem asks for more sacrifice, not for its elimination or substitution, which must intensify one's meditation on war.

It was customary in an earlier age to kill a member of another family to avenge the killing of one's own. Humanity took centuries to free itself from the emotional logic of revenge to devise a way whereby a murderer was tried and sentenced and appropriately punished by a court—a form of substitutionary justice. Society was thereby saved from the chaos of private revenge seeking. If we consider national wars something akin to it—only on a grander scale—isn't it about time nations also settled for justice by substitution?

IV

It was a delicate topic, but I felt safe in broaching it to Professor Baum, a famous Canadian Catholic theologian. It was none of my business, but the best questions have to do with what is none of our business. On second thoughts, perhaps it was my business. In any case, this was my question: how could Christian evangelism be reconciled with the religious freedom of others?

Many answers are possible but I wanted a good Christian answer from a good Christian.

"It has to do with kenosis," he began. "From one point of view, there are three main ingredients to Christianity: God, Christ and the Church. God is perfect, but God had to create room in Himself, to empty Himself for the universe for it to come to be. The key idea here is that of self-limitation."

As he said this, I thought of the Hindu idea of creation as *sṛṣṭi* (letting go). But I let the thought pass.

"Even in relation to us God exercises this self-limitation, this kenosis, not just in relation to the universe. For instance, God is omnipotent but He allows human beings an area of genuine choice to exercise our free will, without which we will be automatons and not human beings . . . so God exercises kenosis. . . .

"Now, Jesus, His son, does the same. Jesus has to empty himself of [a] solely divine nature to assume [a] human nature. This is another manifestation of self-limitation. Just as God voluntarily lets the world be, and the human beings in this world be, Jesus voluntarily foregoes His divine nature enough to allow room for human nature. So Jesus exercises kenosis.

"It is my view that just as God exercises this kenosis, this self-limitation, and Jesus does too, the *ecclesia*, the Church, should follow his example and do the same. Yes, the Church is supposed to evangelize the world but just as out of His love God practiced kenosis, and out of His love Jesus practiced kenosis, then out of its love the Church should practice kenosis."

Was this truly a novel formulation, or did it sound novel to me because I did not know enough about Christianity? I had never heard anything like it before. I was impressed.

"Have you written about it," I asked eagerly.

Professor Baum fell silent for a moment and then said, "No." And then he began to laugh!

Thus it was that the experience of Christianity brought me face to face with the obvious but elusive truth that, even when people of different faiths read the same scripture, they read it differently. Might one even venture the view that they are different—the insider and the outsider—precisely to the degree that they read the same text or perhaps even the same passage differently. Thus, Professor Baum had read the kenotic passages in the Bible very differently from me—but also very differently, I dare say, from other Christians. Yet, his voice was an original Christian voice, because he is a Christian, even though his reading differed from that of other Christian readers. Such differences at one time could even be considered heretical, but now they are considered original. Can one doubt that they enrich a tradition? As the French say, *vive la différence.*

Of course, the French had another kind of difference in mind, so much more radical than within people with the same distinguishing features. But should we take formal affiliations to traditions as constituting such a distinguishing feature, then it is possible to be more radical in the present context as well. Just as the analysis of kenosis was moved in a particular direction by Professor Baum as a believing Christian—it has also been moved in yet another direction by a believing Buddhist. Professor Masao Abe, perhaps the foremost scholar of Zen in its Western context, draws parallels between *kenosis* and *śūnyatā* (emptiness) as understood in Buddhism. Professor Baum is in a state of dialogue with his own tradition; and Professor Abe, in a state of dialogue with another tradition—yet the tradition in both cases is Christianity.

Perhaps, the dialogical component of my experience of Christianity tells us something about Christianity itself and the leadership it has provided in the context of the dialogue of world religions. But this leads us back to the issue we apparently seemed to be moving away from—of how we experience the same texts differently when experiencing a religion, depending on whether we are doing it from within and without.

My first perceptions of the Bible, like Gandhi's, consisted of the calumny it heaps on the unbelievers. His glimpses of other religions in his childhood—specially Islam and Zoroastianism and Jainism were positive:

> Only Christianity was at the time an exception. I developed a sort of dislike for it. And for a reason. In those days Christian missionaries used to stand in a corner near the high school and hold forth, pouring abuse on Hindus and their gods. I could not endure this. I must have stood there to hear them once only, but that was enough to dissuade me from repeating the experiment. About the same time, I heard of a well-known Hindu having been converted to Christianity. It was the talk of the town that, when he was baptized, he had to eat beef and drink liquor, that he also had to change his clothes, and that henceforth he began to go about in European costume including a hat. These things got on my nerves. Surely, thought I, a religion that compelled one to eat beef, drink liquor, and change one's own clothes did not deserve the name. I also heard that the new convert had already begun abusing the religion of his ancestors, their customs and their country. All these things created in me a dislike for Christianity.[8]

The point is that Gandhi, as an outsider—first came to know of its teachings in relation to unbelievers and *then* subsequently its message of love and charity. It is telling that in the very next paragraph he mentions the Hindu text *Manusmṛti*, which left him cold. This provides me with the occasion to say that the first verses of the *Manusmṛti* I became conscious of were the verses which included the pursuit of virtue. It was only when I started studying Hinduism academically that I became aware of the verses within it that are derogatory of the lower classes. It seems reasonable to assume that an outsider becomes aware first of these derogatory verses and then, if at all, of any positive contents of it. The lineaments do not change when the focus is narrowed—as, for instance, on what Manu has to say on women. I first learnt the positive things he has to say about them—that gods dwell where they worshipped. Little did I know of the negative things he has to say until much later.

It is as if we go through three phases in our dialogue with our own tradition: first it speaks to us positively, then it speaks to us negatively, and then we speak to it—positively or negatively as the case may be. Professor Baum provides one example here.

Another example of this last phase is provided by Professor Krister Stendahl. I might be guilty of gratuitous, even potentially narcissistic self-referentially by referring to myself in the above sentence, but by doing so, I wish to invoke my Hindu identity, which in its modern perception, is shaped by the belief that Hinduism is non-proselytizing. My Hindu identity also likes to think it is so by choice, although historians might suspect that it is only making a virtue of necessity—as some claim Judaism did—in the face of the obviously more successful proselytizing religious enterprises like those of Islam and Christianity. The self-perception that it is so by choice, however, often translated into an active aversion toward proselytization and does not, at least any more, stop at mere indifference to it. It is with such a background that I came to Professor Stendahl's exegetical exercise.

The exercise essentially consisted in his taking three biblical passages, which virtually serve as texts for proving Christian missionary activity, and demonstrated that they stand for something else:

> (1) Acts 4:12: . . . for there is no other name under heaven given among human beings, whereby we must be saved.
>
> (2) John 14:6: . . . I am the way, the truth, and the life: no one comes to the Father except through me.

(3) Matthew 28:19: . . . Go therefore and make disciples of all the nations, baptizing them in the name of the Father, and of the Son, and of the Holy Spirit.[9]

The first passage Professor Stendahl contextualizes as follows: "This is Peter's response to the accusation of having performed a miracle in his own name—and what he claims is that it could only be God's work."

The second passage Professor Stendahl contextualizes as follows: "This is Jesus' farewell speech. He says he is leaving, but the followers should not worry for they know the way to the place too. When Thomas doubts whether they know the destination, he allays their fears by becoming a confident lightning rod for them."

The third passage Professor Stendahl contextualizes as follows: "Matthew's gospel is totally built on the theory that, during the ministry of Jesus, neither Jesus nor his disciples were to move outside Israel."[10] But this statement applies to the Gentiles. According to Professor Stendahl, it is the model of Israel which is commended here—an exemplary outpost model, not an all-conquering mission.

The remarkable shift in perspective involved is best illustrated graphically:

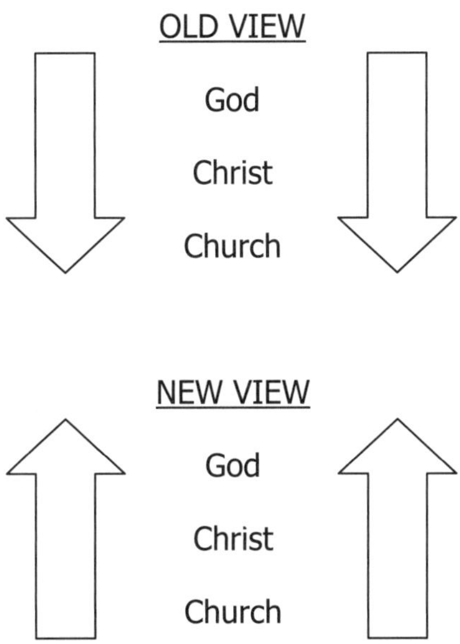

As we saw earlier, the direction makes all the difference.

I may now make a transition from the theological to the liturgical and ask, "Why is a Christ necessary for Christmas?"

I could say that Christmas is no longer a Christian festival. This statement could point in several directions. Some would say it has now become too commercial to be called Christian—the profit-motive has at least supplemented if not supplanted to such a degree the piety motive in its celebration. As a student of comparative ethics, I might be inclined to concur, but as a student of comparative religion I am inclined to demur. In many ways, early Christianity bears a striking similarity to the cargo cults its presence in places like Papua New Guinea has given rise to. These cults believed that the ancestors of its practitioners will soon return with cargo full of goodies they now see in the possession of Christians. There would be reversal of fortunes, quite literally, in the near future. And, the more the tribal people contemplated the prospect, the nearer it seemed—until they were almost possessed by an apocalyptic frenzy, to such an extent were their expectations heightened by their eagerness. The secular phrases, such as "feeding frenzy" or "freight train," in this sense capture the religious sentiment well. This scenario is not unfamiliar to students of early Christianity. In fact, the two are so similar that the early Christian phenomenon could be considered an anticipation of it, or the later cargo cult a repetition of it. In this respect, Santa Claus holds as much the key to our understanding of Christmas as Jesus.

There is, however, another sense in which Christmas is no longer Christian: the sense that it is no longer restricted to the Christian West but has gone global. In the same way in which the seven-day week is no longer just Western—or, if you wish to be historical—Roman, its weekly rhythm is almost global. Christmas is celebrated all over the world. It has almost become a secular festival.

My reflection, however, is less concerned with the global dimension of Christmas than with the universal insight I associate with the "person" in whose name the festival is celebrated. A recent book on world religions commences its chapter on Christianity with a reference to Christmas as follows:

> Throughout the Western world, the year reaches a climax towards the end of December. At that season, Christians celebrate the birth of Jesus, whom they regard as the manifestation of divine nature and purpose in human life. The birth took place in Palestine about 2,000 years ago.

> Christians assert that in Him God had reached out, taking on and conquering humanity's weakness.[11]

Jesus conquered humanity's weakness, humanity's sin, by taking it upon himself. The question I have to ask is: if God's grace is free, and even unmerited, then how does the action of somebody offering himself or herself as ransom for someone else enter the picture?

There is a curious coincidence of opposites here. If one believes in karma; if, as the Qur'an says with karmic rigor, "No one shall bear the burden of another," then in a curious coming together of Hinduism and Islam, no one need atone for someone else. It obfuscates the merits of each case! Because God's grace is *unmerited*, then no one need atone for anyone else for that subverts the very idea of unmerited grace. There is a dilemma here that may be resolved by putting another dilemma beside it in some form of philosophical homeopathy: either God's greatness is such as exceeds our understanding, of which this dilemma is a part, or the dilemma itself is a part of God's understanding which transcends our criterion of consistency.

Whether Jesus' substitutionary atonement makes theological sense or not, I have come to conclude that it makes unimpeachable moral sense. It has to do with the logic of forgiveness as a way out of a moral cul-de-sac.

A central experience of life concerns the question of justice, or, rather injustice. All of us experience it. Children experience it; geriatrics experience it; adolescents experience it; middle-agers experience it. The young experience it, the old experience it. Men experience it, women experience it. Kings experience it; paupers experience it. The great experience it; the small experience it. Individuals experience it; families experience it. Nations experience it; continents experience it. Why go so far away? You experience it; I experience it.

Christianity offers a radically new perspective in this regard—that, *at the fulcrum of the universe, lies justice and not injustice.* Adam and Eve were expelled from paradise into an "unjust" world on account of a transgression—an act of injustice on their part in the eyes of God. We face a very powerful paradox here: that our experience of an unjust world is rooted in the workings of justice.

And, in the Christian understanding, it is the location of our dislocation in justice, which enables it to be overcome through Jesus Christ—the vicarious atonement of Jesus Christ.

Why could God not have simply forgiven? Why did God have to send Jesus Christ to reconcile Himself to humanity?

In order to answer this question—a great question—one has to start humbly—with just two human beings. Let us take the case of two individuals, A and B. Let us now suppose that A hurts B in some way. Then A repents and B forgives A. The matter should end there. It doesn't.

To see why it does not end there, one must grasp the concept of surplus sin. The concept may be presented as follows. When A hurts B, then B is the victim. B has a fund of grievance against A. B is the bearer of this burden. If B forgives A, then B also takes on this burden as well. Thus, B bears a double burden: the original burden of being sinned against and the additional "burden" of doing the forgiving. A goes scot-free.

The unilateralism of the procedure will not be lost upon the reader. The idea of a ransom or a compensation is meant to convert this unilateral process into a bilateral one. For otherwise A could go on sinning against B, and B could go on forgiving A ad infinitum.

One more point. When one seeks *justice*, one seeks to convert a unilateral process into a *bilateral and symmetrical* process. When one seeks *revenge*, however, one seeks not only to convert a unilateral process into a bilateral one; one also introduces an asymmetry in the process by causing another *injury*—the margin by which revenge exceeds justice. This in turn invites retaliation and thus commences an ascending dialectic of revenge-taking, which could also in principle go on ad infinitum.

Thus, both runaway unilateralism, based on lop-sided forgiveness, and runaway bilateralism, based on revenge, must be avoided if an aggrieved relationship is to be restored.

In other words, there can be no complete healing without compensation.

Teaching Islam

I

The phone rang in my claustrophobic quarters in Cambridge, Massachussets. It was a fateful call. It was going to tell me whether I had the job of teaching Hinduism in faraway Australia. I lifted the receiver.

"Is this Arvind Sharma?"

"Yes."

"Are you still available?"

"Yes."

"You have the job. You will be getting all the details officially, but I have a question to ask you."

"Yes, please go ahead."

"Can you teach a course in Islam?"

I paused. I think I had good reason to pause. Here I was, someone who had just been hired to teach Hinduism, and the first question I was being asked was, "Can I teach a course in Islam?" But you can't be rude to someone who has just offered you a job!

"I did take a graduate course in it. . . ."

"It will only be at the introductory level. . . ."

"I think I could do that."

"Cheerio-o."

"Jolly good. . . ."

According to the Hindus, the world is *maya*. The concept can be variously explained, but to say that, "things are not what they seem," may do for now. In that case, the academic world is surely *maya* par excellence. How else would one explain that someone hired to teach Hinduism a moment ago was asked if he could teach Islam the next?

Finally, the day did arrive when the matter became public, that I would soon be teaching a course in Islam.

Brisbane had a local population of Muslims, some of them from the Indian subcontinent. This provides the necessary background for what was to follow. I was summoned by the head of my department one day to take a call. The caller was a Muslim who wanted to sit in the class to make sure I did not misrepresent Islam when I taught it. I asked him to enroll as a student. The outcome of our conversation was inconclusive, and I awaited further developments.

Sure enough, the summons came again from the head, but this time it was not a phone call but for a request for a meeting with the caller himself. And the Muslim began by congratulating me for enabling Islam to be taught in the city!

I do not know to this day what made him change his mind. And all this melodrama even before a single class had been held! So the anomaly of a Hindu teaching Islam apparently was going to persist. In fact, it continued to flourish.

Why this Islamic sensitivity to the prospect of a non-Muslim teaching Islam? Or, perhaps, there are not one but two questions here, embedded in this academic situation: (1) Why is the sensitivity of an insider aroused by the prospect of his or her religion being taught by an outsider? (2) Why is the sensitivity of a Muslim specially aroused by this prospect? Let us here focus on the second for that is how I got involved in the issue in the first place.

I offered the opinion earlier that the sensitivity of the Muslim is *specially* aroused in this respect. But is this a correct statement to make? So it seems. One can hardly visualize local Hindus, Christians, Jews or Chinese or Japanese going on alert if it were announced that courses in their respective religions were being introduced in the curriculum at the university. Or, perhaps, the comparison is not fair. Was it the fact that a Hindu—from the Indian subcontinent with its alleged history of Hindu-Muslim antagonism—was going to be teaching Islam, which aroused the Muslims' suspicions? How would local Jews feel if a card-carrying Nazi was about to give a course in Judaism? The analogy may be a bit overblown, but does it not point in the right direction—namely, that politics might have been involved? When it comes to an Indian Hindu teaching Islam; an Israeli teaching Islam, or a Palestinian Muslim teaching Judaism are the right images to conjure up. The fact that the objection came from Pakistani (and not) Indian Muslims in town perhaps helps, though one must wonder again whether a liberal Muslim *from Pakistan* would be as upset at the prospect as a conservative or fundamentalist Muslim *from India*? So we have here an issue of truly Byzantine intellectual complexity—and this was before the Iranian Revolution. . . .

I was having dinner with Professor Willard Oxtoby of the University of Toronto at the Holiday Inn. He was in town, and we were discussing the fate of religious studies program at our respective universities, which seemed to be perpetually on the block.

I asked him, "How can they think of doing away with religious studies anywhere now, given the role religion is playing in the world?"

"I don't know. But it sure has saved me from having to answer a lot of questions."

"Like how?"

"Like if I would fall into conversation with a fellow passenger sitting next to me on a flight and he would ask me what I did. When he would discover I taught religion for a living he would go, like, what is a nice person like you . . . but you know what? I have never been asked to justify my profession after 1979."

1979, of course! The year of the Iranian Revolution. But I was talking about 1977 here—not just before the *fatwah* (judicial ruling) against Salman Rushdie but before Khomeini had even come to power. . . .

Or is the explanation more profound—and goes back to the origin of the religion itself? After all, Islam is perhaps the most "political" of all religions in terms of its origin. When the Prophet migrated to Yathrib from Mecca in 622 CE, and the city was renamed the "City of the Prophet" in his honor, whence the name Medina (*medinat-al-nabī*). He was welcomed as *both* the religious and temporal head. Judaism was also "political" at birth, but its post-Christian political disempowerment left the Jews (like the Hindus) a people averse to politics until recently. In the Islamic case, however, history providentially favored the early connection, which in turn generated the confident expectation in Islam—until frustrated by the rise of the West in the eighteenth century—that the fulfillment of its global destiny was at hand. It would be fanciful to liken the local protest to either this expectation or frustration, but the higher level of political awareness in Islam perhaps need not be discounted entirely.

Or did the explanation lie elsewhere? Did it have something to do with the "response threshold"?

> A "response threshold" is crossed when it becomes possible for the believer to advance his or her own interpretation against that of the scholar. In classical comparative religion this was hardly a problem, since most of the scholar's time was spent investigating the religions of the past and often of the very remote past. Interpretations might be challenged, but only by other specialists working according to Western canons and conventions. Today, by contrast, a greater proportion of study is devoted to contemporary, or at least recent, forms of living traditions. The study of religions often shades into a dialogue of religions, in which the views of both partners are (at least in theory) equally important. The response threshold implies the right of the present-day devotee to advance a distinctive interpretation of his or her own tradition—often at variance with that of Western scholarship—and to be taken entirely seriously in so doing.[1]

God forbid—a Hindu about to teach the Western version of Islam! This was certainly an opportunity for an insider who was probably already at the response threshold.

II

While on a faculty-exchange in the United States, I was put through a more vigorous test—a course on Hinduism and Islam in India. One could argue that teaching Islam *theologically* in general was a sufficiently clinical and academic exercise and could to be safely undertaken even by a Hindu or a Jew, but teaching it *historically* in the Indian context might pose unique problems when undertaken by a Hindu.

It did but not of the kind I had anticipated. We discussed the partition of India toward the end of the class, and after sharing the various perspectives, I offered the view that, from a purely objective point of view, the formation of Pakistan was a spectacular achievement of Muhammed Ali Jinnah.

I was not prepared for the deathly silence, which ensued. The class included a Sikh and a couple of Muslims. The Sikh was from India. The Muslims were from the Middle East and from Indonesia.

I thought the silence had to be broken. So I continued, "In the end, the Congress and even the British and sizable sections of the Muslims themselves were opposed to it, but Jinnah pulled it off."

The silence only deepened.

I had to change the subject. Acknowledgment does not mean endorsement no more than compliance means acceptance, but the class was not ready to buy it. Or, better still, I had not prepared it to buy it.

The partition of India is an emotional minefield. It maimed the subcontinent and continues to maim others. The mixture of resignation and regret, which characterizes the following comment by a British cultural historian, is perhaps representative of the sentiment of a large number of Indians at the time of partition in 1947, although their proportion has since considerably diminished, yielding ground to those who not only are more resigned to it[2] but also regret it less sixty years later:

> . . . the Muslims with their rigidly codified religion, were too much for even the omnivorous Hindu culture to digest. Interaction between the two religions and ways of life indeed took place, and once at least a modus vivendi was almost reached. It is not wholly surprising, however, that, when India began to reassert herself, two nations should have replaced the single British Raj; but all impartial students must regret that the unity of the Indian sub-continent has been once more lost, and trust that the two great nations of Indian and Pakistan may soon forget the bitterness born of centuries of strife, in co-operation for the common welfare of their peoples.[3]

There are actually at least three major "grand narratives" regarding Indian independence and partition. And one must hear all of them in order to understand the silence of the class.

According to the British version, the British found an India torn apart by "bitterness born of centuries of strife"—between Hindus and Muslims. With great difficulty and considerable self-sacrifice, they established some semblance of law and order on the subcontinent and then proceeded to modernize it, progressively introducing representative government as part of this modernization and trying to involve Hindus and Muslims equally in the process. Although, until the very end, they did their very best to act as honest power brokers between the two, they failed. When they found the subcontinent ripe for self-government, they left—and because the Hindus and Muslims insisted on having countries for themselves, India had to be divided. So, all credit to the British and as for Hindus and Muslims, sotto voce, "a plague on both your houses."

The Pakistani version is different. "The Pakistani may see Indian history as a great Muslim creative achievement superimposed on a corrupt pagan society and culminating in the Moghul period and the reign of Aurangzeb. The British were the darkeners of this light."[4] A darkening in which the Hindus treacherously collaborated. The British basically saw in the Mutiny of 1857 a Muslim effort to end Britain's benign dispensation over India and thereafter took to favoring the Hindus over the Muslims. The two conspired against the Muslims till the very end—and the fact that the Muslim-majority Kashmir should be part of India rather than Pakistan is final proof of this.

The Indian narrative differs from the British and Pakistani narratives:

> The Indian historian is inclined to see Indian history as a splendid Hindu creative cultural achievement leading to a golden age in the fourth and fifth century A.D., followed by the humiliation of Muslim conquest and domination, the British episode, and the glorious renaissance and revival of the last and present centuries.[5]

This account by a historian comes close to summarizing one Indian position,[6] except that, according to the majority view, it underplays British involvement. According to this view, the British may have favored the Hindus as a counterweight to the Muslims until 1900, but once the Indian national movement picked up steam, they were constantly trying to derail it by constitutionally favoring the Muslims and by fomenting Hindu-Muslim differences in general to sabotage the movement toward national independence. When they could not prevent such independence any longer, they contrived to divide the subcontinent before leaving it. The history of British rule over India may, according to this view, be summarized in an epigram as follows: first divide and rule; then rule and divide; and then divide and quit.

III

The opportunity to teach Islam reappeared in Canada as part of an introductory course on the Abrahamic religions. When it came to the teaching of the Islam component—for various reasons, ranging from the academic to the political—all eyes turned to me. All eyes turned to me, and my eyes turned heavenward.

One does what one can, so I did what I could. In order to keep the class interested in the subject, I would conclude each class with a "thought for the day," usually a nugget from Islamic lore.

In the excitement of the final day, I almost forgot to share the thought for the day. The class was beginning to break up when I suddenly remembered what I had forgotten. "Hold it," I exclaimed. "The thought for the day. I have a special one for you—my favorite *hadith* (a saying of the Prophet)."

Everyone came to a stop, as in a freeze-frame. It was rather picturesque and dramatic: just like in the movies. And then I said:

> The ink of the scholar is more sacred than the blood of the martyr.

The fact that the class burst out in spontaneous applause took me by complete surprise—and happy wonderment.

Such was not always the case. Teaching Islam is not always sweetness and light. I discovered this also in a somewhat surprising manner. After teaching the segment of the course on Islam—in which I had covered its origin, history, doctrines, law, and mysticism in broad strokes—I set apart one whole class for questions before we moved on to the study of another tradition. I wondered whether I was being overconfident in doing so, for the questions could literally pertain to anything. However, I rather enjoy being on the firing line, perhaps the expression of a "streak of pedagogical masochism." Besides, nothing boosts the morale of a class on the eve of an exam more than to find that the instructor is unable to answer one of *their* questions!

What took me by complete surprise was the fact that, with one exception, all the questions were on *jihād*, a topic to which I had perhaps devoted fifteen minutes of class time. For one full hour, I fielded the questions on *jihād*—right, left and center—to the point of feeling as if I was myself engaged in one!

The issue of *jihād* is not exactly a new topic, and there are many ways to go about it. And I think I traveled down most of them. I point out that the word *jihād* does not quite mean what it is translated as, namely, holy war. In fact, one needs a separate word in Arabic to translate holy war—*harb-e-mukaddas*; *jihād* means to exert in the way of God (*fī sabīl allāh*). It is true that such exertion can include martial activity, but is not confined to it, as becomes clear from the term *ijtihād*, which is a legal term and denotes exegetical exertion to elicit fresh applications of the law to unprecedented contexts. In fact, just following the five pillars amidst the distraction of daily life can count for *jihād*, while a famous *hadith* distinguished the lower (physical combat) from higher *jihād* (combating negative tendencies within oneself).[7] Indeed:

> . . . the whole of life may be said to be a constant jihād between our carnal and passionate soul and the demands of the immortal spirit within us. It was in reference to this profounder meaning of jihād that the Prophet said to his companions after a major battle in which the very existence of the early Islamic community was at stake, "Verily, ye have returned from the smaller jihād to the greater jihād." And when one of the companions asked what the greater jihad is, he answered, "to battle against your passionate soul (nafs)." Islam, therefore sees jihād as vigilance against all that distracts us from God and exertion to do His Will within ourselves as well as preserving and reestablishing the order and harmony that He has willed for Islamic society and the world about us.[8]

Thus, exertion in the way of God could take many forms: pietistic, legal, and moral as well as martial. And in this latter sense, which so dominates the semantic horizon, it is applied to defensive warfare. One even concedes that the doctrine of *jihād* may have been abused—even used as a fig-leaf to cover naked acts of aggression—but then no doctrine could be judged by its deviations, although such deviation must be factored into its assessment.

And, to balance the perversion of the doctrine, we find creative applications—as when, in Tunisia, pursuing industrialization was defined as *jihād*. During *jihād*, fasting is not compulsory. In this way, factory workers could eat and carry on with the project on hand, lest the fasting of Ramadan lead to an economic slowdown.

But the class kept coming back—as if determined not to entertain any other understanding of *jihād* except this: that Islam divides all people between believers and unbelievers and provides believers with a carte blanche to kill unbelievers. One female student actually said toward the end, "We understand what you are trying to do, but we can't understand how a religion can condone the taking of life."

Finally, I told them the famous story about Hazrat Ali, the fourth caliph. He was engaged in a hand-to-hand combat with an opponent during a *jihād*, when, in the to-and-fro of battle his face came within spitting distance of his combatant, who thereupon spat on it in disgust. At this, Ali immediately dropped his arms. The age of chivalry was not yet over, and the combatant also stopped the fight, wondering why Ali had disengaged. Whereupon Ali explained, "Before you spat on me I was fighting you for the sake of God. If I fight you now, after your having spat on me, I would be fighting you for revenge. That is not *jihād*." This calmed the class down into noble silence, but only for a while, and soon the questions started again! The popular image of the Prophet, with sword in one hand and the Qur'an in the other, seemed impervious to academic assault. I just had to learn to fight my academic *jihād* better.

Stereotypes, if allowed to go unchallenged for too long, become archetypes. It is a tragedy from the point of view of the comparative study of religion that these stereotypes have become so powerful as to acquire a life of their own. They have become so extraordinarily potent as to even cast the evidence—even evidence to the contrary—into their own mold, instead of allowing it to crack the stereotypical mold. Thus, if an Islamic community is at peace, it is presumed to be preparing for a *jihād* or recovering from a *jihād* or having failed in a *jihād*! At this point, the stereotype is no longer falsifiable; in the jargon of the philosophy of religion, it has become a *blik*.

This is bad enough. But what is perhaps worse is that, just when you think you have got the students past their prejudice, just when you sit back in the belief that you have struck a blow for truth, something happens which reactivates the stereotype! Just when you thought you were winning your *jihād* against the misunderstanding of *jihād*, an Ayatollah Khomeini announces a death sentence against a Salman Rushdie! Just when you think you have convinced your class that *jihād* must not be conflated with terrorism, September 11, 2001 comes along. Just when you thought you had tiptoed with your class around the minefield of the misunderstandings of widow-burning in Hinduism, the story of a Roop Kanwar committing *sati* in Deorala, Rajasthan hits the stands. Just when you have succeeded in persuading your class that racism in the United States has virtually no religious dimension, a black church goes up in smoke deep in the south! The academic teaching of religion has its own calamities to contend with.

IV

Like *jihād*, the position of women in Islam is a hardy perennial. It weaves itself in and out in various ways, but the heuristically challenging parts of it pertain to the presence of quadrigyny in Islam and visible gender segregation as represented, in increasing degrees, by *hijāb* and *purdah*.

I decided to try a bit of proleptic pedagogy in discussing the married life of the Prophet and began my lecture that day by asking the students if they thought President Clinton had dated before he married Hillary (as distinguishing from dating after he had married her?). Most felt that he must have. Somewhat surprisingly, the women students in the class were more forthcoming in support of the proposition. Now that I had them where I wanted them to be, I told them how scandalous this appears in the kind of segregated society I grew up in. Such behavior is considered loose and immoral there; did this entitle me to consider President Clinton loose and immoral on this ground? The ensuing silence buoyed my spirits, and I also provided a moment of silent introspection, which descended on the class with the familiar observation that Muslims do not see much difference between the simultaneous quadrigamy *permitted* in Islam and the *serial* polygamy practiced in Western society.

But the most direct refutation on gender oppression they witnessed was at the hands of the Muslim woman student I brought to the microphone, a woman who would have been considered attractive in any religious milieu. At the end of her brief presentation, she finally faced the class and said, "You keep hearing about the oppressed women of Islam. Now look at me. *Do I look oppressed*?" she asked. The class applauded, though a few cries were heard, "But you are in Canada." Her comeback was, "Is the definition of Islam the monopoly of any one country?"

When these approaches are not apologetically obtrusive, they can be heuristically quite helpful—but I still feel that they do not go to the heart of the matter as I see it. It seems to me that every society has to make a basic decision in relation to how it will deal with the biological division of human beings into men and women. In this respect, a fundamental choice may be involved, which may broadly be termed as a choice between integration and segregation. I invite you to consider the concept more than the words, and the social awareness involved even more than the concept. What is most important is the degree of awareness which will be attached to the biological distinctions: These differences cannot be erased, but they can be overlooked as much as possible at the one extreme, and taken as much into account as possible at the other. Very simply then, modern Western society has gone as far as possible in the direction of integration and traditional Islamic society has gone as far as possible in the direction of segregation.

The appreciation of this point is obscured by the fact that each society views its own position as normatively compulsory—with the

West holding itself up as the ideal mirror for Islam and vice-versa. Once this element of missionary compulsiveness is removed from the equation, it does not take long to realize that these societies are presenting us with two distinct models of gender relations.

It is the Western model, which I referred to in shorthand as integration. The crucial point, which needs to be recognized here, is that both of the models—of *integration as well as segregation*—possess some pluses and some minuses, that each model has its benefits and its costs.

The integration model has its benefit in the form of the fullest possible participation of both the sexes in common public life in all its dimensions—ranging from politics to sports. On the other hand, compared to women in segregated societies, it may mean that women will probably suffer more physical violence from the mere fact of the greater contact between the sexes, and the same factor will also lead to more sexual contact between the two—pre-marital, marital and extra-marital, or even platonic. This is not an indictment of such a society or even a criticism. It is merely an observation that, when men and women move and mix freely, this is bound to happen.

The segregation model, on the other hand, narrows the shared ground in civil society between men and women but probably enlarges the sphere of protection enjoyed by women in society. Paradoxically, many Muslim women claim that wearing the *hijāb* has a liberating effect on them—for now others know what behavior to expect from them and to exhibit toward them. Confusion of roles is avoided. (A nun's habit presumably sends a similar signal in Western society). It must not be forgotten that the physical protection of women is a salient element underlying segregation of the sexes, although it may be true that this may have little bearing on "domestic violence," as distinguished from "public violence,"in the two societies being compared.

So, there is a choice involved here. And each choice carries with it a gift, as well as a price tag. In an integrated society, the gift is freer participation in the public domain; the price tag is perhaps a decline in the physical level of public safety of women and in morality in male-female relationships.

These lines were written at least a year prior to the scandal involving the Clinton White House, which has been explicitly used by Islamic fundamentalists to drive home this point. John Stackhouse reports:

> Nestled in one of the most violent quarters of Pakistan's most violent city, Karachi's Banuri mosque swirls with

> revolutionary ideas, and the dreams of young students from around the world.
>
> And what a terrible world it is, Mufti Nizamuddin Shamzi tells them.
>
> Television, he says. It must go. It gives a false image of man. "There is comedy, nudity. These are not needed."
>
> Crime, he continues. It is best treated with retribution. Kill a killer. Maim a thief.
>
> And women, he goes on. They do not belong in public.
>
> *"Contact between men and women should not be allowed in offices."* Mr. Shamzi explains, before succumbing to his own sense of comedy and allowing a half-smile to peep through his thick greying beard.
>
> "Look at Clinton."[9]

In a segregated society, the gift is relatively greater protection from physical violence and less opportunities of friendships between the two sexes becoming more than. The price tag is the public invisibility of women.

This is not meant as a comment on how the individuals in these societies behave qua individuals. There will be men and women with overactive glands in both societies. The ultimate outcome in this regard in each society will involve both the individual units—that is, individuals in the respective societies—and the ways the societies are structured, integrationally or segregationally. The penetrating question to ask is: "To what extent does the structure account for the outcome, and to what extent do the individuals account for the outcome?" My point is that, if we assume normal random distribution of disposition at the individual level, the respective structures of these societies could then be taken as accounting for the variation all the way from the level of public to pubic interaction.

If this assumption is reasonable, then modern Western and traditional Islamic societies offer a genuine choice in this respect. This means that, when Islamic societies choose to live the way they do, their behavior represents not cussedness but a form of choice, and the same applies to the West. We may prefer one model over the other. Most of the readers may prefer the Western over the Islamic. This is their privilege. But I hope this discussion has brought a new element to the table: like the other choice, our own choice has both its costs and its benefits. When we prefer one system over the other, we are preferring one set of benefits and costs over another. The others are doing the same in making their choice. The choice is not between light, all light, and darkness, all darkness. It is more like a choice between the sun and the moon. The sun has its spots, and the moon has its spot. (I shall not enter here into an esoteric astronomical argument of which pattern, integration or segregation, conforms to which landscape, solar or lunar. The fact that, in the wake of the Clinton scandal, female enrollment in evangelical colleges rose should remind us that the issue is not purely theoretical and does not only play itself out only in terms of grand civilizational narratives.[10])

V

The problems we have just discussed relate to the *sharī'ah* (Islamic law). It is virtually customary in liberal circles, both within and outside Islam, to denounce it. Yet, the fundamentalists find it necessary to impose it whenever they come to power. What is going on here?

It seems to me that we are caught here in a conflation between shadow and darkness. The many reactionary provisions of the *sharī'ah* are regularly trotted out to show the dark side of Islam, but they really constitute only its shadow side. Permit me to explain my point.

Islam is the youngest of the major religions of the world and also one which has been spectacularly successful. In this sense, then, it is a missionary religion par excellence. Some have even argued that there is no separate word for missionary in Islam, which only goes to demonstrate that being a missionary is inseparable from being a Muslim. The argument is not correct, but the conclusion is. Islam is ipso facto missionary and is to be classified, along with Buddhism and Christianity, among the great missionary religions of the world.

The moment one places Islam in the same box as Buddhism and Christianity, however, it is difficult not to be struck by a peculiar fact. Buddhism and Christianity were in some ways reformist departures from their "parent" religions—Hinduism in the case of Buddhism and Judaism in the case of Christianity. Now, what did their reformist component precisely consist of? It consisted of jettisoning the deadweight of the law that becomes a drag on the moral and spiritual impulses of these parent religions. In this respect, Islam provides a striking contrast: not only does it *not* represent a reformist splintering from another *major* tradition; rather it provides a firm legal structure to its original followers, who lacked one, and an alternative legal structure for the other civilizations it moved into—unlike Buddhism and Christianity, both of which seem quite willing, as religions, to accept the legal framework of their host civilizations! This generates a monumental contradiction: Buddhism and Christianity became great missionary religions by steering clear of legal structures, while Islam has become a great missionary religion by at least possessing and even offering a legal structure.

Another consideration deepens the contradiction. The kind of legal minutiae, which characterizes the *sharī'ah* in Islam, also characterizes the great *ethnic* religions such as Hinduism, Judaism and Confucianism! In this respect, Islam is more like the great ethnic religions in opposition to whom the missionary religions, such as Buddhism and Christianity, historically took their stand.

Where there is contradiction, there is confusion, but where there is confusion, there is scope for insight. We have now arrived at the threshold of such an insight, but one more step needs to be taken before the threshold can be crossed. The great reform missionary movements often reveal a weakness: when confronted with *another* major missionary movement, or with the resurgence of an ethnic religion, they tend to lose ground. Christianity lost out even in its birthplace when Islam moved in, and Buddhism in many countries yielded rather quickly to the secular missionary movement of communism. Remarkably, by contrast, Islam has held its own against communism.

All this leads irresistibly to the conclusion that, when it comes to spreading, Islam is like a missionary religion, but when it comes to consolidating its hold, it is like an ethnic religion. But how? Through its *sharī'ah,* which enables it to penetrate the life of its followers with the thoroughness of an ethnic religion. In the valid move to change such items of the *sharī'ah* as may seem dated, one should not lose sight of this vital larger reality. I might conclude by succumbing to a cliche: beware of throwing the baby away with the bathwater.

Discovering Zen

I was far away from home, as far as I could get, when I was first introduced to Zen. At the time, I was studying in the United States, halfway around the world from my native India. I had just become friends with a fellow student, who admired the fact that Hinduism did not seek converts. I had always admired this same sense of missionary self-sufficiency about Judaism, so one might say that we were predisposed to befriend each other.

"Are you coming to the talk by Alan Watts?" she asked me.

"Who's he?"

"Someone who writes on Zen, you know," she said in a matter of fact way.

"What's Zen?"

Her demeanor changed to one of mock seriousness.

"You had better come with me," she said, grabbing my arm as she took me to a meeting in the Braun Room of the Harvard Divinity School.

The opening statement was made by Professor Harvey Cox. It took the form of a description of the encounter of the Bodhidharma with the Chinese Emperor, upon the Bodhidharma's arrival in China from South India. It went somewhat as follows:

> . . . the first great personage Dharma [i.e. Bodhidharma] had an interview with when he came to China was the King of Liang, the greatest Buddhist patron of the time. And the interview took place in the following manner:
>
> The Emperor Wu of Liang asked Dharma:
>
> "Ever since the beginning of my reign I have built so many temples, copied so many sacred books, and supported

> so many monks and nuns; what do you think my merit might be?"
>
> "No merit whatever, sire!" Dharma bluntly replied.
>
> "Why?" demanded the Emperor astonished.
>
> "All these are inferior deeds," thus began Dharma's significant reply, "which could cause their author to be born in the heavens or on this earth again. They still show the traces of worldliness, they are like shadows following objects. Though they appear actually existing, they are no more than mere non-entities. As to a true meritorious deed, it is full of pure wisdom and is perfect and mysterious, and its real nature is beyond the grasp of human intelligence. Such as this is not to be sought after by any worldly achievement."
>
> The Emperor Wu thereupon asked Bodhidharma again, "What is the first principle of the holy doctrine?"
>
> "Vast emptiness, and there is nothing in it to be called holy, sire!" answered Dharma.
>
> "Who is it then that is now confronting me?"
>
> "I know not, sire!"
>
> The answer was simple enough, and clear enough too, but the pious and learned Buddhist Emperor failed to grasp the spirit pervading the whole attitude of Dharma.
>
> Seeing that there was no further help to be given to the Emperor, Dharma left his dominion and retired into a monastery in the state of Wei, where he sat quietly practicing the "wall contemplation," it is said, for nine long years, until he came to be known as the Pi-kuan [i.e. wall-contemplation] Brahman.[1]

I wasn't quite certain as to what was going on, even after the meeting was over. My friend was deeply disappointed in Alan Watts on account of what she thought was a "sexist" remark he had made. (Did it mean the same as "sexy" or was it different? I did not know at the time.) I didn't know what was going on to have any views about anything at all. In retrospect, it wasn't such a poor introduction to Zen after all! Small wonder many would laugh when I would ask them earnestly: "What is Zen?"

It soon became apparent, however, that Zen had something to do with Buddhism, and further, that it was a form of Buddhism, and then further, that at least for some it was Buddhism itself.

This shook me. I had always fancied myself to be a Buddhist. Modern Hindus love to do that, but I had even gone beyond that and even occasionally harbored the conceit that I had been a Buddhist monk in my past life. And here was a Buddhism I did not even know about. But I kept this "in my heart," the way Mary kept Jesus' words when she couldn't understand them.

All things come to them that wait—including Zen masters—especially in Cambridge, Massachusetts. This meeting was billed to take place at the Center for the Study of World Religions at Harvard University. I didn't miss it, but it almost missed me. The Japanese master spoke through a translator and mostly cracked jokes, one pleasing me in particular perhaps on account of the fact that I had recently abandoned the study of economics. He wisecracked that "companies started by economists invariably fail!" In hindsight, this might have been a subtle way of insinuating to us the limitations of book learning in relation to religion, but at the time it was just a good joke.

Zen is nothing if not dramatic. For right there the Japanese visitor, before our very eyes, drew a depiction of a bulbous-eyed monk in black on a white sheet of paper. It was christened "Bodidharma arriving from the West" and continued to adorn one of the walls of the Center for some time.

It was quite an experience, which brought me face to face with my delusions of adequacy. I had thought I knew Buddhism, but obviously what I knew was the Theravada form of Buddhism, specially as it had flourished in Sri Lanka. It's the Theravada texts I had read as Buddhist texts; it's the Theravada life of Buddha, which I knew to be the Buddha's life. Of course, I knew that Buddhism had spread over much of Asia; what I was now beginning to realize was that I knew little of the various forms it had assumed in the course of this journey. I had so far been the proverbial "frog in the well"—but I was ready to see the ocean.

That this broadening of my horizons should be taking place in the United States initially perplexed me. The United States does not exactly possess a reputation for religious virtue in the rest of the world. And yet, in the heart of Massachusetts, I was discovering the treasures of the religions of the world, to quote Keats, like "magic casements, opening on the foam Of perilous seas, in fairylands forlorn." From the frothy tabloids of Harvard Square to the magic casements "on the foam" in Divinity Avenue was a ten-minute walk! In due course, I was to realize that D.T. Suzuki had arrived in the United States around the same time as Swami Vivekananda, around 1883, that is. I knew next to nothing about Suzuki and almost all a "Hindu nationalist" needs to know about Swami Vivekananda. I had a long way to go to complete my education.

II

A major step in this direction was taken when I began to teach comparative religion at the University of Queensland in Brisbane, Australia. Queensland, I learnt only later, had the reputation of being the backwaters in Australia, a status curiously confirmed by the fact that the sale of *Playboy Magazine* was banned in this part of Australia at the time.

You can then imagine my surprise when, in this global remoteness, I discovered students interested in Tibetan Buddhism. A Tibetan Buddhist monastery was functioning in the more remote part of even Queensland. I could only admire such missionary zeal, though not the conditions of living there, which were too spartan for someone like me having the time of his midlife, as best as I could, in Brisbane. Some of my students were the living manifestation of the Buddhist presence, which also included Zen.

Later, the portals of the Zen temple were finally pushed open for me by Masao Abe. By then I was teaching in Canada, and through his good offices, I was able to spend some time at the Zen Center in San Francisco, while he was teaching at the Pacific School of Religion. He was a living practitioner of Soto Zen and traced his lineage, through Hiramatsu, back to Dogen—the founder of Soto Zen.

And thereby, hangs a story, which told me more about Zen than anything since. Buddhism offers the philosophical insight with nothing less than absolute certainty that certainty (or truth) can be less than absolute; but it is when this austere doctrine gets embedded in an autobiographically rich life like that of Dogen that its bones put on flesh. It seems that Dogen had apparently despaired of attaining enlightenment, in pursuit of which he had undertaken his trip to China, and was about to board a ship home when he learnt that an enlightened master, Ju-ching, was residing at a nearby monastery. So, in the spirit of giving it one more try, he decided to join the master's meditation.

Ju-ching was rather severe in insisting on meditation and especially impatient with those who fell asleep during a meditation session. Even when someone urged exhaustion as an extenuating circumstance, Ju-ching would hear nothing of it. He replied:

> Absolutely not. Those who do not possess the mind for the Way would fall asleep in the Meditation Hall even if the sitting period was shortened. For those who have the mind for the Way and the determination to discipline, the longer the sitting period, the greater enjoyment they find in their training. When I was young, I went to visit abbots in all corners of the world. One of them once told me, "If a monk was sleeping, I used to strike him until my fist nearly broke. I have grown old and weak now, and I cannot strike as hard."[2]

The account continues:

> It was during one of those moments when Ju-ching was admonishing a disciple not to fall asleep during the meditation session that enlightenment came to Dogen. One day during the intensive summer training (*hsia-an-chu*) in the first year of Pao-ch'ing (1225), Ju-ching shouted at a disciple, "When you study under a master, you must drop the body and mind; what is the use of singleminded intense sleeping?" Sitting right beside this monk, Dogen suddenly attained a Great Enlightenment (*ta-wu;* Ja. *Taigo*). Immediately, he went up to the abbot's quarters and burned incense. Ju-ching inquired, "What is the burning of the incense for?" Dogen replied, "The body and mind have been dropped." "You dropped the body and mind!" said Ju-ching approvingly. In humility, Dogen said, "It might have been a momentary delusion; please do not give me the Seal [of approval] indiscriminately." Ju-ching assured him, "I do not grant you the Seal indiscriminately." Dogen pursued the point, "How can you say that you do not grant the Seal indiscriminately?" Ju-ching replied, "You indeed have dropped the body and mind." When Dogen made obeisance to Ju-ching, the attendant Kuang-p'ing from Fu-chow, who was sitting beside Dogen, exclaimed, "This man from a foreign country attained the Great Matter. This is indeed not a trifling matter at all." Thereupon, Dogen left humbly.[3]

As is well-known, there are two main traditions of Zen—the Soto and the Rinzai. My special admiration, apart from a general fondness for the tradition, is reserved for the founder of Soto Zen as an individual, but when it comes to method, for the methods of Rinzai

Zen. The use of the koan is associated with this Rinzai tradition. These koans have the subliminal power to stop the mind. In this sense, they are the opposite of the mantra, which literally means an instrument, or shall we say, a blueprint of thought. The word *koan* also means a blueprint, but it is a blueprint to stop thought. In the long run, of course, the ultimate goal of the mantra is also to transcend thought, but the koan's immediate goal is to stop it. Consider the thought-stopping quality of koans like the following:

> A master, Wu Tsu, says, "Let me take an illustration from a fable. A cow passes by a window. Its head, horns, and the four legs all pass by. Why did not the tail pass by?"
>
> Or again: What was the appearance of your face before your ancestors were born?
>
> Another: We are all familiar with the sound of two hands clapping. What is the sound of one hand clapping? [If you protest that one hand can't clap, you go to the foot of the class.]
>
> One more: Li-ku, a high-ranking officer of the T'ang dynasty, asked a famous Ch'an master: "A long time ago a man kept a goose in a bottle. It grew larger and larger until it could not get out of the bottle any more. He did not want to break the bottle, nor did he wish to harm the goose. How would you get it out?"
>
> The master was silent for a few moments, then shouted, "O Officer!"
>
> "Yes."
>
> "It's out!"[4]

If then thinking is the most subversive form of activity according to the rationalists, then not-thinking is even a more subversive act according to Zen—as it even subverts the logocentrism of rationalism. I first felt the impact of the Zen perspective, outside of the study of Zen itself, in a course on the philosophical aspects of Advaita Vedanta. One of the central foci in the modern formulation of this school of Hindu thought is represented by the question: Who am I?[5]

It has been very helpful for me to treat this mantra, Who am I? as a *koan* to assess its claim to soteriological potency within Advaita Vedanta.

Over the past few years, this convergence between the techniques, or even statements, of Zen masters and the masters of Advaita Vedanta has grown increasingly teasing. For instance, it is a cardinal assumption of Zen Buddhism that all human beings possess Buddha nature; and the question whether all living beings, including dogs, possess it, has given rise to a famous koan:

A monk asked Joshu, a Chinese master: "Has dog Buddha-nature or not?" Joshu answered, "Mu." [Mu is the negative symbol in Chinese, meaning "no thing" or "nay."]

It is now that the remarkable nature of the following observation of Ramana Maharshi becomes apparent. While conversing with an inquirer:

> . . . at one stage, he said laughing: "These all, each one of them is a Buddha. But they do not know it. If they would only know that they were Buddhas, always, there will be no problem."[6]

The Eastern position in relation to religion—specially as it surfaces in systems as close or as far apart as Zen and Advaita Vedanta—does not have to be accepted. But I think it has to be appreciated. And what has to be appreciated is that both of them, as systems of religious thought, are acutely conscious of the fact that they are systems. They recognize this limitation, and for that reason alone, I think worthy of our respect, for to be conscious of one's limitation is to have already exceeded it. In religion, this distinction is vital, as vital as not mistaking the menu for the meal.

This does not imply that everything is relative, and hence anything goes even if nothing arrives. It might help here to distinguish among three kinds of relativism. Let me first label them as inevitable relativism, relative relativism, and radical relativism—and then explain them as follows.

The prevalent idea, which often associates relativism with "anything goes," could serve as an illustration of radical relativism. An example might help. It is like looking at an object, such as a TV set and saying that all the views we can have of a TV are relative and, therefore, have the *same* value or lack of it. This is radical relativism.

Another extreme is represented by the same realization but in a difference sense—that a totally objective view of the TV set is impossible because to look at it from anywhere at all is to look at it from somewhere. Situatedness is, thus, inevitable; it is inescapable. This I call inevitable relativism.

Let us now introduce the consideration that, for certain purposes, some angles of looking at the TV set might be relatively better, in the sense of being more suitable for the matter on hand, like watching a

TV program. Some angles for watching a TV screen are better than others. This belief I refer to as relative relativism.

When we say, "Everything is relative," it could mean any of these three things. Zen, as a system of thought, displays its maturity by recognizing inevitable relativism as inevitable. However, at the same time, it resists the temptation to absolutize the relative, a view we described as one of radical relativism. Then, consistently with the middle way of Buddhism, it offers itself as an approach to salvation, which some might relatively find more useful.

III

It was in the summer of 1997 that I had my first opportunity to visit Japan—a land I had admired for long from a distance. The reader may not be able to go along with my reasons for this admiration, but I hope he or she will still feel that it is at least a reasoned admiration and perhaps also a reasonable one. My admiration is rooted in the belief that, of all the countries of Asia, Japan provided the most cogent, perhaps even the only cogent, response to Western imperialism. It also seems to be the one culture that has distinguished "modernization" from "Westernization," most perceptively in favor of the former.

Once I had settled down at the International House in Tokyo, I came down for dinner, with all the tentativeness of a foreigner in a new country. After I had given the order, which was taken with customary courtesy, I felt more relaxed and looked out of the window. A small placid lake greeted my sight, set off by adjoining rocks and foliage. The light of a lantern was reflected in it. As my eyes moved away from it I espied the calm reflection of a lunar disc in the still water, as lucidly as in a mirror. There was an aura of perfection about it. The following lines then flashed forth from the dark unknown recesses of my memory:

> The moon is reflected deep
> inside the lake
> Yet the water shows no
> sign of penetration!

At that moment, I really felt that I was in Japan. And, strange as it must sound, I also felt, far as I was away from home, I was also home. And, then, it began to dawn on me that the lines I had so effortlessly recalled were as koanesque, as the scene they described was picturesque.

Religions of India and China: Caught in the Middle

I

China and India—two cultures with the longest continuous histories in the world and perhaps, on that account, used to considering themselves, if not the center of the world, then at least central to the world—both calling themselves the middle-country, with all the ambience that goes with being at the center of it all. Already, by the second century AD, India had appropriated the status of a *jagadguru* (a world teacher) for itself. The *Manusmṛti* says (11.20):

> From a Brāhmaṇa, born in that
> country, let all men on
> earth learn their several usages.[1]

China was not to be left behind. Yiching, the Buddhist pilgrim who visited India toward the end of the seventh century, writes:

> The people of the five parts of India are proud of their own purity and excellence. But high refinement, literacy elegance, propriety, moderation, ceremonies of welcoming and parting, the delicious taste of food, and the richness of benevolence and righteousness are found in China only, and no other country can excel her. . . . In the healing arts of acupuncture and cautery and the skill of feeling the pulse, China has never been superceded by any part of India; the medicament for prolonging life is only found

> in China. . . . From the character of men and the quality of things China is called the "Divine Land." Is there any one, in the five parts of India, who does not admire China?[2]

As Jawaharlal Nehru, India's first prime minister, noted some years before he rose to that position: "India might be the 'noble region' but China was the 'divine land.' "[3] We have seen earlier that, not to be outdone, India had staked a similar claim. Earlier on, Faxian, who visited India in the fifth century had felt differently: "He sadly called to mind the imperfections of the monks in China and prayed that in future births he might be born in India alone."[4]

II

When Xuanzang returned to China after his prolonged stay in India, in 645 CE, the Chinese emperor himself received him in person. When he asked him what he intended to do next, Xuanzang basically said "more translating"—of Sanskrit texts into Chinese. And the emperor's suggestion that some Chinese texts might be translated into Sanskrit for the benefit of the Indians left Xuanzang unmoved.

The Indians of today—struggling to create a viable independent political state—must wonder if the outcome might have been different if the proposal had fallen on fertile soil and if the Confucian classics had been translated into Sanskrit? Would they have played as important a role in the political thought of India, as the translation of Buddhist texts in the religious thought of China? I do not wish to imply that India has no tradition of political thought of its own. But I do wish to suggest that Indian political thought, apart from some flashes of it in the *Arthaśāstra*, never quite engaged in sustained reflection on the nature of a state with a strong center, much less nurture it. The genius of China, at least pre-Communist China, was personified in the mandarin, that of India in the Brahmin. However, the ease with which the idea of an elite administrative service was adopted from China and adapted to run India by the British so successfully, does make one wonder if an Indian imperial mind might not have taken the cue long ago. "No ancient Indian state . . . developed a trained bureaucracy and efficient control of regional bureaucrats by its central administration."[5] Might this verdict not have been different?

India never evolved a proper bureaucracy, unlike China; China never evolved a proper alphabet, unlike India; yet, when they met across the frontiers, they did not help supply each others civilizational needs—although Samudragupta did adopt the title of Son of Heaven (Devaputra),[6] and the monk Shou Wen did try to "develop an alphabetical system along [Indian] lines."[7] Both of them took hesitant steps in each other's direction, but none of them went far enough.

III

My immersion in Confucian thought produced an unexpected side effect in terms of how I came to view the study of comparative religion. This requires some explanation.

The study of religion—especially if one approaches it as a quondam, or current, or would-be "philosopher"—exerts its fascination as a possible avenue for the discovery of truth of some kind. Each worldview excites with the promise of what it might disclose about the universe, about us, and about the ultimate reality we did not know, and it excites us all the more that such disclosure may not only provide some novelty in relation to the views already held but that it might even disclose *the* reality, or at least a reality.

The reality I speak of here is reality of the universe, not the reality of religion. The study of religion is, no doubt, deeply involved with the reality of religion itself, of the historical reality of a religious tradition, the global reality of religion in any age, and of religious phenomena. Is the ultimate reality about religion religious? Is what people think their tradition teaches the same as what their ancestors thought it taught? What were people's religious beliefs around the world like in the fifteenth century? Is another person's experience of his or her tradition unique, and how close can I come to experiencing it? Can I do so without converting to the other religion? In any case, what patterns can I detect in these data? All these are engaging questions, but they pale, it seems to me, before the questions: Did Yahweh really promise Canaan to Abraham and those who came after him? Is Jesus really the Son of God? Are the words of the Qur'ān really God's words, literally? But even these questions begin to take second place in the presence of questions which delve even deeper—beyond the reality of the individual religious traditions to the reality itself—questions about the ultimate reality about things. It was after all in trying to find an answer to the questions about ultimate reality that the various specific answers came forth like shining crystals.

When one surfaces after immersion in Confucian thought, however, with its focus on location and situatedness, one looks at the world with a slightly different gaze. The world is the same, but the gaze is different. For one begins to wonder whether *temperament may not have as important a role in generating a worldview as truth.* As a prelude, let us consider this simple point—that liberals and the orthodox are found in virtually all religions, so also conservatives and radicals. To a certain extent, these dispositions can perhaps be correlated to the teachings of a religion, but I think it is fair to ask, in the light of the virtually universal distribution of such temperamental differences, as to whether the temperament itself does not predispose one to accepting or rejecting a certain teaching, or interpreting it in a certain way.

"A Sufi has rightly said: 'No understanding of the Holy Book is possible until it is actually revealed to the believer just as it was revealed to the Prophet.' "[8] But the believer is not the Prophet, not in the sense that the line of verbal prophecy terminates with the Prophet but in the sense that no two individuals are alike. The understanding of the truth of the Qur'ān, or rather of the truth through the Qur'ān, is bound to be colored by the temperament of the receptor. I do not imply any distortion here, only a difference in the quality of reception, just as how one sees a picture is affected by where one is standing. Again, it is not an issue regarding pollution and purity; but it is a point regarding location and reception.

At this point, the discussion will now move beyond Confucianism only to return to it later. For now, the issue has broadened into one of temperament in general. How does temperament affect truth? The concept of objective truth implies that truth, in some sense, is beyond temperament, that the truth of scientific data depends on the accuracy or inaccuracy and not on the geniality or irascibility of the scientist—although how the truth is offered to us, cordially or sullenly, does depend on temperament. The question becomes more complex once the trajectory of truth travels past the sentinels of scientific objectivity. At the moment, however, one might pause with the recognition of this complexity and pursue the point further at the lower level of the presentation of data pertaining to the religious life of a human being itself at a particular moment in the process.

One could then propose to present such data not in terms of a religious tradition—or a time-period,or a theme—but also in terms of temperament. One could, for instance, press into service the fourfold classification of psyche proposed by Jung as a typology of the human personality and use them as four markers for organizing the data; or alternatively, one could take one's cue from the fact that "there are, according to the Hindu analysis, four general kinds of persons. Some are basically reflective, others are primarily emotional. Still others are essentially active. Finally some are most accurately characterized as empirical or experimental. For each of these personality types a distinct yoga, is recommended. . . ."[9]

These yogas, of course, are Jñāna Yoga, Bhakti Yoga, Karma Yoga and Haṭha Yoga. In other words, the religious data can be organized in accordance with these four yogas.

At this point, the question arises: What does one hope to gain by such a procedure? Any reorganization of data on fresh lines usually holds the promise of yielding new insights. What precisely these insights are going to be like it is not always possible to foresee. The insights that the organization of religious data according to themes disclosed is well-known to all students of the phenomenology of religion, even though it might not have been possible to anticipate them when the new approach was first tried. In this particular case, however, at least a part of the benefits might have been foreseeable. When data are organized according to the yogas, then one likely result is going to be a deepened and broadened understanding of a particular yoga. This will have the effect of making the academic study of religion an ally in the active pursuit of religious life, in the same manner in which science is allied to technology. The gulf between the academic study of religion and the practice of religion could, thus, be partially bridged.

An actual example will help clarify the point. Under which rubric will most of Confucianism be placed in the schema of the four yogas? A little reflection will reveal that, of the four, the most appropriate place for it would be under Karma Yoga. For Karma Yoga covers the field of social and ritual activity. Yet, the very act of placing Confucianism under Karma Yoga becomes immensely consequential for the nature of Karma Yoga itself—at least in two ways. The general understanding of Karma Yoga until now has primarily been in terms of ritual (as with the Mīmāṁsakas) or ethical action (as with the *Bhagavadgītā*). Now, although Confucianism contains elements of ritual, it is primarily as a system of social relationships that it lays claim on our attention. Thus, Karma Yoga now obtains a more clear-cut *social* dimension than it has hitherto had. One may not know how this ties back with the emphasis in the *Gītā* on one's *varṇa* duties or calling. Yet, this is not where the emphasis per se lies in the *Gītā*—it is on the non-attachment to the rewards of the action performed. But Confucianism places the emphasis on the social duty *itself* and, thus, lights up as this facet of Karma Yoga in its fullness. This emphasis in turn will not be entirely sterile in its impact on Karma yogins in modern India.

IV

My first awareness of the Chinese sages derives from seeing them ensconced in the Hindu pantheon at the Birla Mandir in Delhi. It was, therefore, with more than usual interest that I read the following passage with which A.L. Basham concludes his entry under Hinduism in *The Concise Encyclopedia of Living Faiths*:

> Typical of the new Hinduism is the Lakṣmīnārāyaṇa Temple at New Delhi, commonly known as Birla Mandir after the prominent industrialist who endowed it. Birla Mandir is not by any means a great work of art. Its architecture and sculpture are uninspired and largely traditional in style. But it preserves within its courts some of the wonderful mixture of ebullient vitality and mystical calm which is typical of the best of India's religious art. In Birla Mandir there is no question of excluding untouchables and non-Hindus; the temple gates are open to all who wish to enter. Here not only are the gods of Hinduism worshipped and the great saints and doctors of Hinduism reverenced, but room is found for the chief teachers of other faiths and lands also—Jesus and Muhammad, *Confucius and Lao-tzü*, Plato and Aristotle. The earth itself, which has mothered the millions who over four thousand years have built up the civilization of India, is revered in a shrine where a map of the Indian sub-continent replaces the usual image. Birla Mandir is symbolic of the new Hinduism—a vigorous faith with a deep social conscience and considerable missionary zeal, willing to accept whatever it deems good wherever it finds it.[10]

So, a religion that once thought it stood at the center of the earth has overcome its dilemma by making the earth stand at its center! But this involves more of a geographical than an ideological orientation, for, when viewed in Hindu terms, Confucius and Lao-Tzu seem to symbolize the two paths to engagement in and disengagement from the world—the paths of *pravṛtti* and *nivṛtti*, the two paths laid out in the Vedas, which Śaṅkara refers to his prefatory remarks on the *Bhagavadgītā*:

> The Twofold Vedic Religion
>
> The Lord created the universe, and wishing to secure order therein, He first created the Prajāpatis (Lords of creatures)

> such as Marīchi and caused them to adopt the Prav*ritti*-Dharma, the Religion of Works. He then created others such as Sanaka and Sanandana and caused them to adopt the Niv*ritti*-Dharma, the Religion of Renunciation, characterized by knowledge and indifference to worldly objects. It is the twofold Vedic Religion of Works and Renunciation that maintains order in the universe. This religion which directly leads to liberation and worldly prosperity has long been practiced by all castes and religious orders (varna-āsrama)—from the brāhmaṇas downwards,—who sought welfare.[11]

The *Bhagavadgitā* itself then tells us how to be a Lao-Tzu on the inside, while one is a Confucius on the outside! In one respect, however, the teachings of Lao-Tzu seem to differ, although in a rather subtle way, both from the *Bhagavadgītā* in particular and Hindu theism in general. Thus, both the *Bhagavadgītā* and the *Tao Te Ching* counsel equanimity, but there seems to be a subtle difference in the approach they recommend to achieve this in the face of the vicissitudes of life. The equanimity recommended by the *Bhagavadgītā* seems to be more akin to that of a rock that weathers all storms in its solidity. The equanimity recommended by the Taoists is more like water that accommodates itself to every situation. In one, you remain unshaken; in the other, you rise with the crest and roll with the punches (to mix metaphors).

Nevertheless, the end gained is the same. Yet, although the ideal is the same, the ideal person is still somewhat differently conceived, and the difference is telling. That the Chun-Tzu—the noble person described by Confucius—is not averse to playing a political role should not surprise anyone, but given its Confucian proximity, even the pure crystal of Taoism reflects the royal hue:

> In the human sphere the *Lao Tzu* describes the perfect individual, the sage, who comprehends this mystic principle of Tao and orders his own life and actions in accordance with it, humbling himself, pursuing a course of quietude and passivity, free from desire and strife. *It is clear that the sage is conceived of as the ideal ruler, for the Lao Tzu gives definite instructions as to how the sage is to conduct his government.* He is to cease from meddling in the lives of the people, give up warfare and luxurious living, and guide his people back to a state of innocence, simplicity, and harmony with the Tao, a state that existed in the most ancient times before

> civilization appeared to arouse the material desires of the people and spur them to strife and warfare, and before morality was invented to befuddle their minds and beguile them with vain distinctions.[12]

There are flashes of this in Hinduism in the concept of *rājarṣi* (the royal sage), but then the concept fades away as the distinction between the Brahmin and the *kṣatriya*, the priest and the king, is formalized and takes hold—so much so that even in Buddhism the destinies of being a universal monarch and a Buddha become optional destinies.

In Hinduism, then the ideal of a *cakravartin* (world conqueror) remains just that, an ideal, while in China there are historical approximations of it (on the ethnocentric assumption that China and India themselves constitute the "whole world" for all practical political purposes. Did Alexander have to set out to conquer the world because Greece was so small?)

If Confucianism provides contrasts in relation to Hinduism, then Taoism suggests similarities. The French savant, Louis Renou was not beyond suggesting and even borrowing on that basis:

> As regards the influence of China, if the admittedly striking parallelism between the techniques of *Yoga* and those of Taoism lead us to assume that one borrowed from the other it would seem that the initiative must be attributed to India: for it is in India that the tradition is most firmly established. If certain texts call Tantrism the 'Chinese practice,' *Cīnācāra*, the term refers to Tibet as the region from which *Vajrayāna* was diffused; it does not imply that so profoundly Indian a movement had its roots outside.[13]

But similarity may not necessarily imply borrowing and certainly does not imply identity. Consider how a Taoist peasant counsels, and a Hindu king is counseled, to deal with adversity. First the case of the Chinese farmer whose horse ran away.

> His neighbor commiserated, only to be told, "Who knows what's good or bad?" It was true, for the next day the horse returned, bringing with it a drove of wild horse it had befriended. The neighbor reappeared, this time with congratulations for the windfall. He received the same response: "Who knows what is good or bad?" Again this proved true, for the next day the farmer's son tried to

> mount one of the wild horses and fell, breaking his leg. More commiserations from the neighbor, which elicited the question: "Who knows what is good or bad?" And for a fourth time the farmer's point prevailed, for the following day soldiers came by commandeering for the army, and the son was exempted because of his injury. If this all sound very much like Zen, it should; for Buddhism processed through Taoism became Zen.[14]

Compare this with the following story of the presumably Hindu king who cut his hand. The parentheses relate to the swami who is narrating this story to a couple who have just been involved in a car accident.

> There was a King. He had a Minister. Whenever the King said anything—whatever he said—the Minister would say, "That's good!" (*acchā huā*). Whatever happened, he would say, "It was good that it occurred." ("You might have heard this story," Swamiji looks up at Govindbhai standing at the foot of his chair, "to say that whatever happens is good?" Govindbhai smiles, nodding. In fact, most of the rest of us have heard this story, too, for it is one of Swamiji's favorites.)
>
> One day the King went to hunt somewhere. One of his toes was cut off. In his assembly, he said, "One of my toes was cut off."
>
> "That's good" said the Minister.
>
> "What kind of idiot is this?" said the King. "He's my Minister and when I tell him my toe was cut off he says that's good! I'll dismiss him," he said.
>
> "You're sacked from your job," he said.
>
> "Very good," said the Minister.
>
> "Go home!" he said (loud and abrupt).
>
> "That's very good." (Swamiji agreeably rolls his head, voice level and resigned.) He went home.
>
> The King remained silent. He had sent the Minister home. Things continued like this, and then in a few days the King went out hunting. The Minister wasn't around so he took the army (*senā*) with him. Night came. The King went off in one direction, the army went off in the other. The tribal people (*janglī log*) there captured the King. They

captured him, and they have a custom for what they catch: the custom of offering sacrifice. "We've got a nice goat," they thought. They were going to offer him to their god. They have a tribal god (*janglī devatā*). They look out for a good day, those people. After finding this day, all the people of the jungle get together for a big function. They play all kinds of instruments, then they slaughter something. After slaughtering it, everyone takes away a little consecrated food (*prasād*).

They planned this celebration (*utsav*). "Just today we found him." They planned to slaughter him. They decorated him, they played instruments. They said: "You're going to be slaughtered and offered as a sacrifice. We will offer you to our god."

There was nobody to free him. Just as goats are taken (for sacrifice), he was being led forward, with a garland around his neck and instruments playing. He was weeping. But who would free him? He was King only in his own house. Now tribals were taking him.

There, from inside the priest (pujārī) was coming forward, dancing like this: (Swamiji sits upright to wave his right arm above his head, torso swaying.)

There was a big sword in his hand. He came and looked at the King.

"So this is the animal!"

("You understand what I mean by 'animal,' don't you?" Swamiji laughs, "Goat!" Govindbhai, nods, smiling.)

He walked round the King three times, holding the sword. The garland had already been put on. He was sprinkling water on the King. He looked at the king from top to bottom. He saw that on his foot, one toe had been cut off.

"Where did you get him from?" he asked (tone indignant and eyes fierce behind spectacles).

Those people asked (voice dropping into surprise), "Why? We brought him from just over there."

"This won't do!" he said (loud again). "He's been cut once before. Something that's already been cut won't do for our god. It can't be offered to Bhagavan. He's already been cut once. Let him go!" he said.

Once he said the King should be released he couldn't be offered. So they set him free.

When the King was freed he thought, "My life was saved!"

(Swamiji is laughing, and the rest of us join, relieved.)

He went and sat on his throne. After he sat there, he called for his Minister. He had been saved because his toe was cut off, right? So he remembered the Minister. He called that same Minister who had said that before. He gave the job back to him. "Come brother, what you said was very good. You said it was good that the toe had been cut off. My life was saved. Yes? This was good. And you said it was good."

(Govindbhai is called next door for a long distance call from Bombay. "I'll be right back," he tells Swamiji. Swamiji looks after him hurrying out the door. Then after a pause, Swamiji continues for the rest of us present. He fixes his eyes on Govindbhai's wife. She sits on the women's side of the room, nodding her head.)

"You said it was good, and it was good. Then when I dismissed you from your job you said it was very good. What was very good for you in that? You were sent home. You said it was good that my toe was cut off; you said it was very good that you were dismissed from work. What's very good about losing a job? What was very good about that?"

The Minister said, "Maharaj, what happened is this: I said it was very good because you and I were always together. Your toe was cut off. We would have wandered there together. Those people let you go because your toe was cut off. But my toe isn't cut off. They would have let you go but caught hold of me. I would have been offered as the sacrifice. Because you let me go, my life was saved too. That's why I said it was very good."

(A pleased murmur of laughter rises through the room.)

Both of them were saved! (Swamiji beams.) It's good, it's very good.

Whatever Bhagavan does, there's always some reason or the other.[15]

Is this stoicism of the story of the Chinese farmer to be traced to Taoism and the optimism of the royal story to Hindu theism?

Rediscovering Mahatma Gandhi

I think it was Mahatma Gandhi's grandniece, who first gave me an inkling that Mahatma Gandhi was held in some, even considerable, esteem even in the United States. I had then not visited America but was about to. When we met over dinner, she told us how she had endless requests to speak on Gandhi while she was in the States, and I wondered if I might also be called upon to do so while there. She gave me a withering look: "I also have the Gandhi name," she said. And to think that someone might wonder what's there in a name! What lay behind millionaire Birla's unceasing donations to the Gandhi cause? He just could not get over the fact that an Indian could be so famous! "Whom did we have to look up to of our colour when we were growing up"—a black ministerial candidate was to confide to me—"but two people: the Emperor of Ethiopia and Mahatma Gandhi."

I revered Gandhi in India but discovered him in the United States. In fact, it is also there that I discovered that I revered him. I overheard my wife describe me to someone as an admirer of Gandhi. A wife's assessment of her husband must always be taken seriously. She knows me better than anyone else, even myself. It was like being told that I breathe. I do it all the time without being conscious of it. And when one is told, one knows. Could this respect be because for six years I served as a civil servant in Gujarat—Gandhi's home state in India? I can recall emerging from the room where he was born in the city of Porabandar overwhelmed with emotion, even if any attempt to specify that emotion would be futile. I felt so many emotions. I had thought this was my private reaction until years later I heard a fellow Indian, who was then teaching in Australia like me, describe his experience. I then discovered that, however personal my experience had been, it was not private—he had been similarly overcome. (Did the fact that both of us were historians make a difference? But we were historians of *ancient* India!) Apparently, to the people of my generation, Gandhi was just a part of life even though he died when I was eight years old. I remember the day. We sat at the dining table, "like hungry children gathered around the mother" (in the inimitable phrasing of the Hindu text) to be told who he was, that he was no more, to maintain a minute of silence and pray in our hearts.

For Indians, Gandhi is Moses and Jesus rolled in one. Like Moses, he led us into the promised land, barely living long enough to see us shepherded into the stockade. Like Jesus, he died for God.

But what could he mean to the Americans in the United States or Christians in the West?

When the film *Gandhi* was screened in Australia, I discovered it in the best way possible, through direct experience, from the dentist's secretary, in whose esteem I rose, at least momentarily, the moment she learned I was from Gandhi's country and from my Jewish colleague's sobbing over the movie after nearly not going to see it, (many Jews did not see the film because Gandhi had not approved of the formation of the State of Israel in Palestine). It was that same outpouring of admiration for a man of God.

A man of God? But I revered him because he led us to freedom from British rule. Even after the British had successfully disarmed the country, he was able to rouse us to fight nonviolently and successfully against them. Of course, I know too much of history to attribute this freedom to him alone, but people of his stature become symbols of the whole set of circumstances, which secures an outcome. I noticed a subtle distinction in the Indian and Western admiration of the man: to someone like me, the use of nonviolent means to secure freedom, given our political situation, was a masterstroke, but to his Western admirers, the use of nonviolent means per se was the stroke of the master. They were less excited than we Indians were about the freedom part of it; more were turned on by the nonviolent part—while, in the Indian case, the order of preference is usually reversed. In fact, it came as a rude surprise to me that some Americans were quite ho-hum about freedom from the British! I had thought that, since both America and India challenged and ultimately overcame British imperialism (though we took, shall we say, a little longer), this would provide a historical tie, which would bind us. Not quite. (This bonding comes more naturally with the Irish. An Irishman even shocked my father by telling him that what struck him most about Indians was that we did not hate the British like they did.)

I have long wondered about this lack of solidarity on part of the average American with India. Is it a matter of race? Is blood thicker than even the polluted, if holy, Ganges water?

Let me atone for the potentially racist implication of the foregoing remark by pointing out how crucial the contribution of Americans has been to the beatification of the Mahatma. I will cite only two names—those of Webb Miller and Will Durant. Let me now explain why.

The story of Gandhi's salt satyagraha is well-known—too well-known to be recounted here. But how many have paused to consider why it is so well-known, despite a ban on press coverage by the British government? Because an intrepid Yankee reporter, with the American gift for insubordination, made his way to the site and left behind this unforgettable (and to many Indians unforgivable) eyewitness account of what transpired:

> Mme. Naidu called for prayer before the march started and the entire assemblage knelt. She exhorted them: "Gandhi's body is in jail but his soul is with you. India's prestige is in your hands, you must not use any violence under any circumstances. You will be beaten but you must not resist; you must not even raise a hand to ward off blows." Wild, shrill cheers terminated her speech.
>
> Slowly and in silence the throng commenced the half-mile march to salt-deposits. A few carried ropes for lassoing the barbed-wire stockade around the salt pans. About a score who were assigned to act as stretcher-bearers wore crude, hand-painted red crosses pinned to their breasts, their stretchers consisted of blankets. Manilal Gandhi, second son of Gandhi, walked among the foremost of the marchers. As the throng drew near the salt pans they commenced chanting the revolutionary slogans, *Inquilab Zindabad*, intoning the two words over and over.
>
> The salt-deposits were surrounded by ditches filled with water and guarded by four hundred native Surat Police in Khaki shorts and brown turbans. Half a dozen British officials commanded them: The Police carried *lathis*—five foot clubs tipped with steel. Inside the stockade twenty-five native rifle-men were drawn up.
>
> In complete silence the Gandhi men drew up and halted a hundred yards from the stockade. A picked column advanced from the crowd, waded the ditches, and approached the barbed-wire stockade, which the Surat

> Police surrounded, holding clubs at the ready. Police officials ordered the marchers to disperse under a recently imposed regulation which prohibited gathering of more than five persons in any one place. The column silently ignored the warning and slowly walked forward. I stayed with the main body about a hundred yards from the stockade.
>
> Suddenly, at a word of command, scores of native police rushed upon the advancing marchers and rained blows on their heads with their steel-shod *lathis*. Not one of the marchers even raised an arm to fend off the blows. They went down like "ten-pins." From where I stood I heard the sickening whacks of the clubs on unprotected skulls. The waiting crowd of watchers groaned and sucked in their breaths in sympathetic pain at every blow.
>
> Those struck down fell sprawling, unconscious or writhing in pain with fractured skulls or broken shoulders. In two or three minutes the ground was quilted with bodies. Great patches of blood widened on their white clothes. The survivors, without breaking ranks, silently and doggedly marched on until struck down. When everyone of the first column had been knocked down, stretcher-bearers rushed up unmolested by the Police and carried off the injured to a thatched hut which had been arranged as a temporary hospital.
>
> Then another column formed while the leaders pleaded with them to retain their self-control. They marched slowly towards the police. Although everyone knew that within a few minutes he would be beaten down, perhaps killed, I could detect no signs of wavering or fear. They marched steadily with heads up, without the encouragement of music or cheering or any possibility that they might escape serious injury or death. The police rushed out and methodically and mechanically beat down the second column. There was no fight, no struggle; the marchers simply walked forward until struck down. There were no outcries, only groans after they fell. There were not enough stretcher-bearers to carry off the wounded; I saw eighteen injured being carried off simultaneously, while forty-two still lay bleeding on the ground awaiting stretcher-bearers. The blankets used as stretchers were sodden with blood.[1]

I always read this passage to my classes on Gandhi, despite the fact that I have never, so far, succeeded in reading through it without yielding to emotion at some point, no matter how hard I try. Who was this diminutive man, one has to wonder, who could make men and women of dust, perform such gigantic deeds of staggering valor? Was he right that nonviolent struggle requires a measure of courage far surpassing its more martial manifestation?

Will Durant visited India in the 1930s, while working on the first volume of his *Story of Civilization*—a multi-volume work which, along with his *Story of Philosophy*, was destined to make him virtually a household name in America.

That happened to be the time when India was in the thick of its struggle against British rule, and the British were doing all they could to besmirch India's reputation in order to justify their continued rule over India. This propaganda war was being conducted as fiercely in the United States as in Great Britain and India. The great problem for them was Gandhi—a living repudiation of every scurrilous civilizational accusation that could be leveled against India.

Will Durant took one look at the scene upon arriving in India and saw through it all in one laser-like glance. He was so affected that he *suspended* work on his volume to produce a book entitled *The Case for India*. In this book, he addresses and refutes all the arguments that could be marshaled in support of British rule. It was also during this period that the book *Mother India* by Katherine Mayo was published in the United States It went though several impressions and projected such a negative impression of India on the American mind that this view has not even yet been disabused. But Will Durant did his best to undo its effect in the first volume of his *Story of Civilization*, entitled *Our Oriental Heritage*.[2] He also offered the following assessment in contrast to the verdict of *Mother India*:

> India was the motherland of our race and Sanskrit the mother of European languages. She was the mother of our philosophy, mother, through the Arabs, of much of our mathematics, mother through Buddha of the ideals embodied in Christianity, mother through the village community, of self government and democracy. Mother India, in many ways, is the mother of us all.[3]

In my first year at the university, I overheard my father read this passage aloud to my mother. (He used to raid my library occasionally and had got hold of the book during one such raid. I of course used to raid his library regularly.)

So, it is not out of lack of gratitude that I wonder why Americans don't thrill to our struggle against British rule but rather out of rectitude. Do they admire Gandhi because his renunciation reminds them of their own George Washington, who went back to the farm after leading them to victory? A quintessentially Gandhian act.

Nevertheless, even if the reasons for Gandhian reverence on part of Indians and Westerners might differ in complexion, the basic inspiration remains the same—an aspiration for the "higher life." Perhaps, the admiration of the Westerner is even less unequivocal, because for the Indian, on the halo around Gandhi there sometimes falls the shadow of partition.

Some felt strongly about partition and what ensued—one felt so strongly that he did not hesitate to assassinate Gandhi, and Gandhi did not protect himself from being assassinated. Some then think that Gandhi's charisma is tainted by the partition, and a colleague, at his provocative best, proposed a book with the title, Gandhi: Father of Pakistan. What was Muhammad Ali Jinnah then, only a son of India?

Another colleague, of a different persuasion, joined a band of nonviolent defenders around the Babri Masjid during an earlier unsuccessful attempt to storm it. When the youths, wearing saffron bandannas, reached them, they demanded to know who these old-fogies were. "We are Gandhians," they were told.

"And we are the followers of Godse."
"But he killed Gandhi."
"Yes, unfortunately not soon enough."

To compare Gandhi and Nathuram Godse is to carry shallowness to new depths—or is it? There is a play being screened both in India and among Indians abroad—which upholds Godse over Gandhi. Is it too far-fetched to compare this with the sense of disillusionment with the nonviolent campaigns of Martin Luther King, Jr. which now seems to pervade the black community? Is there a fundamental flaw in the technique of nonviolence: an inability to stand up to *unorganized* violence? In India, Gandhi could nonviolently challenge the coercive power of the state, which had a monopoly on violence, exercised formally through visible institutions. But Gandhian methods were less effective in countering random violence initiated by the Muslim League in favor of Pakistan. Is unorganized, or rather deliberately nonorganized violence, the Achilles heel of nonviolence? Blacks can face down governmental oppression, but can they withstand random acts of racial violence any better than Gandhi's men could stand up to pro-Pakistan guerrilla terrorism?

"Who was responsible for partition?" I asked a noted American scholar of Indian Islam before he retired.

"The British," he said, without a moment's hesitation. "And they are trying exactly the same trick in Hong Kong!"

So, it was with more than normal interest that I watched the ceremonies when Hong Kong was finally handed over to China.

Some years earlier, I had had another conversation, this time with a Pakistani. Life has lost its capacity to surprise at my age, but this conversation came close. "Why was India partitioned?" he asked me. I was first thunderstruck and then dumbfounded. Finally I said, "You tell me. We always wanted an undivided India."

The moment passed. So did several years. We now lived in different cities. The film *Gandhi* had by now been released and was making the rounds.

I was awakened by a phone call at a somewhat unusual hour early in the morning. It was my Pakistani friend. His voice was hoarse. "I saw the film Gandhi last night. You are a historian. I want to ask you something. If the British had said 'no go' to Pakistan, what then?" I paused long and hard. Maybe, I even swallowed hard. Then I said, "This is a very vexed question, but in my view, in that case it wasn't going anywhere—'mission unaccomplished.' "

I could be wrong. But the point to ponder here is not my infallibility but my friend's sensibility. If such was the posthumous charisma of Gandhi, what happened in real life? Why could the Hindus and Muslims not scramble home together? After all, religion in politics could be used in different ways—as a spark to start a fire, as Jinnah did, or as a torch to lead people forward, as Gandhi tried. For the secularists, of course, both were playing with fire.

"Why can't India and Pakistan get along," my American neighbor had asked me, soon after my arrival in the States.

How could I make him see the nonrational dimension of the issue?

"Suppose," I said, "all the blacks got together and said they want a chunk of America for themselves. They just couldn't get along with the whites. And suppose, further, that you had not succeeded in throwing the British out, and through what you thought were their machinations, a Black America was carved out of and established beside a White America. What kind of relations will you have with it?"

He mulled it over for a moment in silence. "Not very friendly, I guess," he finally said and both of us burst out in laughter.

This conversation must now be supplemented with another, which I had with a colleague in Indian studies, soon after the German reunification. But one needs to build up to it. At my age, I claimed earlier, there is little left in life to surprise me, although, I also said earlier, my Pakistani friend's question regarding the raison-d'etre of Pakistan came close to it. The conversation I was about to relate comes close to tying with it.

"Now that Germany is unified, what are you doing about the reunification of India and Pakistan?"

I wondered where his tongue was when he said this. It seemed to be in the right place.

"Are you not overlooking something," I ventured.

"Like what?"

"Religion, for one," I said.

"Oh no." he brushed the question aside with a wave of his hand. "I have worked in the region all my life. The practices of the Hindus and the Muslims are all the same, only the names are different."

I thought again of my Pakistani friend, still resenting the division of Punjab. I thought of the reckless breakneck speed at which the country was partitioned. Was it a case of divorce in haste (even before marriage!), to repent at leisure? I reflected, "All that it had done was to convert India's national struggles into international wars—with still no stable outcome." And when I found myself in India during the fiftieth anniversary of independence, the papers talked less about independence and more about partition. As an Indian, I felt like a criminal returning to the scene of crime—and the crime was partition.

Was the partition of India inevitable? Perhaps it is the wrong question to ask. The question one should be asking is: *is* partition inevitable?

Apparently, Gandhi did not think so. I am inclined to believe that he had chosen Bengal as his theater of activity during the closing years of life not by accident but by design—and the design was to demonstrate that, if the partition could be undone in Bengal, it could be undone in the Punjab. There was even a precedent for it. Bengal had been partitioned in 1905, and that partition had subsequently been annulled.

While I was in India, I had more or less *unconsciously* accepted partition as a fact of history (although consciously I might question it). Then, however painful, it was a fact of history. I am now more inclined to look upon it as a painful fact of history, without the implication that nothing can be done about it, for history is an unceasing process. I now feel that historians have a great genius for making history appear inevitable; they are perfect at predicting the past! The more I delve into the actual events, the more I realize they represent a range of several possible outcomes. Is it difficult to imagine the grandeur of the outcome of what might have emerged from the coming together of the oldest religious civilization of the world, with all the wisdom of age, and the youngest religious civilization of humanity, with all the energy of youth?

This is why I felt cheated on the fiftieth anniversary of India's independence.

PART III

Montreal and After

I had by this time moved to Montreal and begun teaching at McGill University. I had also bought a small apartment for myself although against friendly advice. I had been warned that because of Quebec's periodical agonizing over its role in Canada, which was expressed through referenda, property investment in Montreal was no longer what it used to be.

I remember the moment well when I entered the apartment because I had just returned from a trip abroad and didn't expect to hear the message I did. It was a long message from Professor Harvey Cox. He wanted me to let him know if I was willing to be part of a project on religion and human rights.

Religion and human rights? Aren't they kind of far apart?—I mused. Moreover, isn't human rights just a moral fig leaf Western imperialism still wears, although it has trouble keeping it in place? My misgivings, however, seemed a bit unconvincing to me at the time, as I was conscious even as these thoughts crossed my mind that my reaction was based not on knowledge but on impressions I had formed. If the truth be told, any talk of human rights by the West would be considered laughable in certain circles I knew. I learnt later that the attitude had a solid basis, although it carried criticism to the point of risible scepticism. While human rights discourse was evolving in the West, people in the rest of the world were in the process of being deprived of theirs. It would be facetious were it not so serious a matter.

I was, however, now *in* the West and was now being invited to the table. Should I beware of the Greeks even when they bear gifts, or should I not look a gift-horse in the mouth? Or should I, if they are made of wood, get suspicious?

The invitation presented me with that classic paradox of life: was this a temptation or an opportunity? Has this paradox ever been resolved except in retrospect?

Do we really know why we take a particular decision when we do? Nevertheless, the more I mulled it over, the more I felt drawn toward it. The fact that it involved working with Professor Harvey Cox, with whom I had studied with and then remained in congenial contact over the years, added the mysterious equation of personal relationship to the decision. And one aspect of the invitation attracted to me specially—our unit was to explore the *positive* implications of religion for a human rights discourse. This appealed to me.

Our consultative group—one of four—met in Boston. Other meetings followed. I gladly accepted the challenge of preparing the first draft of our deliberations.

After it had been read and commented upon came the most likely but least expected question: what about the caste system?

The question could not be ignored. It was raised by a black scholar whose grandfather had been lynched trying to educate the "negroes."

This set me thinking. It was of course possible to overlook such "negative" elements in the kind of exercise we were undertaking, but that would be cheating. The investigation of the positive could not proceed without a look at the negative, however different the final print might appear after passing through the transformation of numerous drafts.

I was, thus, forced to reflect on the caste system and forced to think about it in a way that would make sense to my Western colleagues.

My first task was to make the caste system intelligible—neither acceptable nor damnable but simply intelligible—to Western minds. As the raison d'etre of caste is birth-ascription, I asked myself the following question: which cultural (as distinguished from natural) dimension of human existence in the West is defined by birth?

The answer came slowly but was self-evident when it came: nationality. In the West, one's national citizenship is just as firmly based on birth as is caste. This concept is almost religiously binding. Couples from Hong Kong had been known to travel to Canada, with the wife in advanced pregnancy, so that their child could be born in Canada. The child would then a natural citizen, who can, upon reaching the designated age, sponsor his or her parents as immigrants! Birth-ascribed nationality can make a child "the father of the man" in a way Wordsworth could not have imagined. It was worth noting that a child born to U.S. citizens in the United Kingdom is automatically a British citizen, even if the parents are not entitled to hold British passports. Such is the miracle of birth in a modern polity. Although citizenship may be acquired, birth still has priority, as is manifest in the eligibility requirements for the U.S. presidency. The place of birth, then, constituted a *political* space in Western civilization.

A citizen of a country is likely to marry a citizen of the same country and is likely to mix primarily, although not exclusively, with fellow citizens of that country when overseas. In other words, the circle of connubialism and commensalism also tended to be constituted by one's nationality, just as in the case of caste. To a lesser extent, one's predilection toward a certain career orientation also seemed associated with nationality, as revealed by expressions such as Yankee ingenuity, German technology, British diplomacy, etc. Nationality thus provided the proper analogue for caste with this important difference: the place of birth, in terms of caste, constituted a *social* space.

There were other similarities as well. Notwithstanding the hierarchy *among* castes, all are born equal *within* a caste. There is perfect democracy, and one is even judged by one's peers. Caste also constitutes one's social security net, just as the nation, with its social services, constitutes a citizen's safety net. Indians have no social security number; they have their caste.

The popular imagination, especially in the West, overwhelmingly connected caste and hierarchy within a society. The case of nations is similar, however, although outside rather than within each nation. Nations rise to and fall from power. Political pundits who speak of a Third and Fourth World were merely replicating the fourfold *varṇa*, or class order of Hinduism, which subsumes all castes, just as the four worlds subsume all the countries of the world. One would also consider the fact that India perceived itself as the world to such an extent that no classical Hindu "universal" monarch invaded any country outside India, prevented from doing so, we were assured by the Greeks, "out of a sense of justice." The *varṇa* system, said to be characteristic of India, was equated with the world.

The conclusion emerged that both citizenship and caste membership were determined by birth, although differences developed when this shared starting point was worked out respectively in terms of *society* and in terms of *polity*. When applied societally, the birth determinant gives rise to the caste system. When applied politically, the birth determinant gives rise to the nation-state. In both Indian and Western societies, the principle of birth determination was applied at a particular point in time. This point is unknown in the case of India.

In the West it followed the Reformation. Application of the principle produced comparable results, in keeping with respective social and political idioms. Being stateless and being casteless were comparable misfortunes.

The emergence of India as a nation provided an important illustration. To begin with, the weakness of the Indian concept of nation-state has often been remarked. However, when large numbers of people are organized as a society in terms of caste, many of the functions of a state come to be handled socially. Such functions included, to some extent, aspects of the administration of justice. Empires rise and fall; society continues, as it has in India. Whence, from a modern point of view, followed the inadequate politicization of a people, and the weakness of national feeling. Second, while politically organized groups are involved in an *external* hierarchy of nations, socially organized groups based on caste are involved in an *internal* hierarchy. The former is fluid, and the latter is more or less fixed, at least in broad terms and for longer periods than the political eras of nations. Third, the direct relationship between the citizen and the state is mediated by a caste in societies organized by caste. In India today, the competing ideal of a nation has been placed alongside caste, although both are based on birth. The government is attempting to convert all Indians into one caste: the Indian caste.

India is caught, then, in the shift from "society" to "polity." Inasmuch as the latter form of organization is very different from the former, India seems adrift. However, inasmuch as both are based on birth, India possesses a home ground advantage. In cases of both caste system and nation-state, the scale has created the phenomenon, and the basis of the phenomenon in both cases is birth ascription. With this example, I went on to illustrate that, when the principles of otherwise apparently antithetical systems are uncovered, radical revision may be possible. A scalar shift in the operational locus of the basic premise of the caste system renders it "rights-friendly." Do I not destroy my enemy, Abraham Lincoln is believed to have asked, if I make him [or her] a friend?

One fact about premodern Indian history now became a point of interest—namely, that in ancient India, diverse peoples moved around the land of India with surprising ease. The evidence from the Vedic period has to be conjectural, even speculative. Some have proposed that the reason why the *ṚgVeda* does not contain evidence of a trans-Indian origin of Aryans may lie in the fact that the Aryans did not perceive themselves as entering a new country—new territory perhaps but not country.[1] India as a geographic unity is a later construction. Even after the dimensions of *Bhāratavarṣa* (India) had been established by the time of the *Arthaśāstra*, there was virtually no restriction on people roaming across the land from one kingdom to another. In fact, in ancient India, people voted with their feet; if they did not like the rule of a king, they moved on. It seems there was no "legal way to remove a bad king,"[2] and peasants protested against oppressive taxes by exercising this "traditional freedom" to "move away."[3] This may explain the fact that has puzzled some, that "there is no recorded uprising in pre-Muslim India after the Vedic period, i.e., for almost two millennia."[4] Foreign visitors to India seemed to confirm this state of affairs. Faxian, the Buddhist pilgrim, traveled through India in the fifth century during the Gupta period, when in all probability Candragupta Vikramaditya was on the throne. The (surprised?) Chinese observed that people didn't register with magistrates (as was presumably the case in China) and came and went as they pleased.[5] The same seems to hold true for South India according to the evidence provided by the French visitor, Abbe Dubois, who visited that part of India in the eighteenth century. He writes:

> Although amalgamated in some degree, each of these tribes still preserves to the present day the language and mode of life peculiar to the place from which it originally sprang. The same thing may be remarked throughout the Peninsula but especially in the Tamil country and in Mysore, where many families of Telugus are to be found whose ancestors were obligated for various reasons to quit their native soil and migrate thither. The remembrance of their original birthplace is engraved on the hearts of these Telugus, and they always carefully avoid following the peculiar usages of their adoptive country. Yet they are invariably treated with the perfect tolerance. Indeed, every native of India is quite free to take up his abode wherever it may seem good to him. Nobody will quarrel with him for living his own life, speaking what language he pleases, or following whatever customs he is used to. All that is asked of him is that he should conform generally to the accustomed rules of decorum recognised in the neighbourhood.[6]

Abbe Dubois' testimony is particularly interesting because it takes us to the heart of the matter—perfect freedom of physical movement combined with complete preservation of ethic diversity. The point then is that—while on the one hand caste provided a social space, which was closed—it went hand in hand with a territorial space which was open. If one takes Rammohun Roy into account, this sense of freedom of territorial movement across India was apparently taken for granted until ca 1800 in regions as far apart as South India and Bengal. He enthusiastically wrote to the French minister about his impending visit to France, only to be told that he must first obtain a passport. Roy was shocked that a country which gave the world the slogan of equality and fraternity, should ask for a passport. A portion from his letter to the French minister protesting the requirement bears citing. He wrote in the third paragraph:

> Such a regulation is quite unknown even among Nations of Asia (though extremely hostile to each other from religious prejudices and political dissensions), with the exception of China, a country noted for its extreme jealousy of foreigners and apprehensions of the introduction of new customs and ideas. I am, therefore, quite at a loss to conceive how it should exist among a people so famed as the French are for courtesy and liberality in all other matters.[7]

The Hindus, thus, took both the restrictions imposed on their social movement by the caste system and the lack of any restriction on their territorial movement for granted.

The concept of territorial citizen presents a mirror image of this situation. All citizens in the modern nation state are free and equal citizens of it, but they are not free to acquire the citizenship of another country, at least not without losing their own. Thus, caste and country offer a curious alliance of opposites. I might even say that they represent two versions of a prototypical system—one social, the other political.

So, if we want to abolish the caste system prototypically—then let all restrictions on marriage among castes be removed in theory and practice (as in India) and let all restrictions on movement from one country to another—all restrictions on emigration and immigration—be removed among all the countries of the globe.

It will probably help us see this comparison between casteism and nationalism clearly if we tried to plot it on an imaginary map. Let us imagine a plain surface. On this plain surface, let us draw a baseline and call it India or Europe. On this baseline, let us set up well-defined rectangular blocks side by side. Each one of these could then be named after a European country such as the United Kingdom, France, and Germany. Please note that the citizens within each country have similar dietetic preferences and intermarry freely. They also have distinct languages and cultures and are ethnic entities in the sense that their membership is based on birth. Note that, while there is immense social, political and economic activity within each unit, there is relatively little across it (although this picture may now have to be modified after the formation of the European Union).

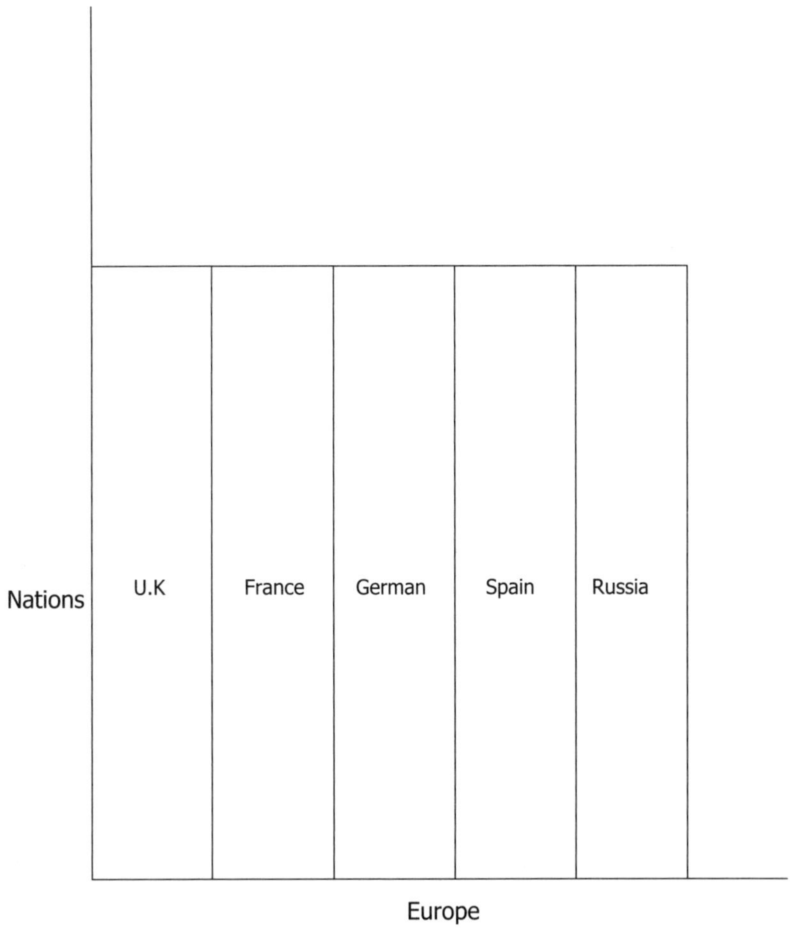

Alongside this diagram, let us draw another as part of our continuing exercise in imaginative cartography. Now, we drop a straight line on an imaginary surface, a vertical line, as opposed to the horizontal line we drew in the previous exercise. Now imagine several rectangular blocks extending out to the right from this line.

They also have the shape of imaginary rectangles. They could then be named after a caste, just as in the previous exercise the blocks were named after nations. Let the first one be called Brahmins; another below them, the martial castes; yet, another below it the Baniyas; and so on. These units are also like the nations in that they share culinary habits, tend to marry among themselves, may have their own distinct languages in different parts of India and are characterized by cohesive social and political activity and, to a lesser extent, economic activity. Thus, while there is a lot of activity within these blocks, such activities across the blocks are not very pronounced. One more act of imagination will complete the picture. It is to draw a horizontal line from the base of the vertical line and label it India.

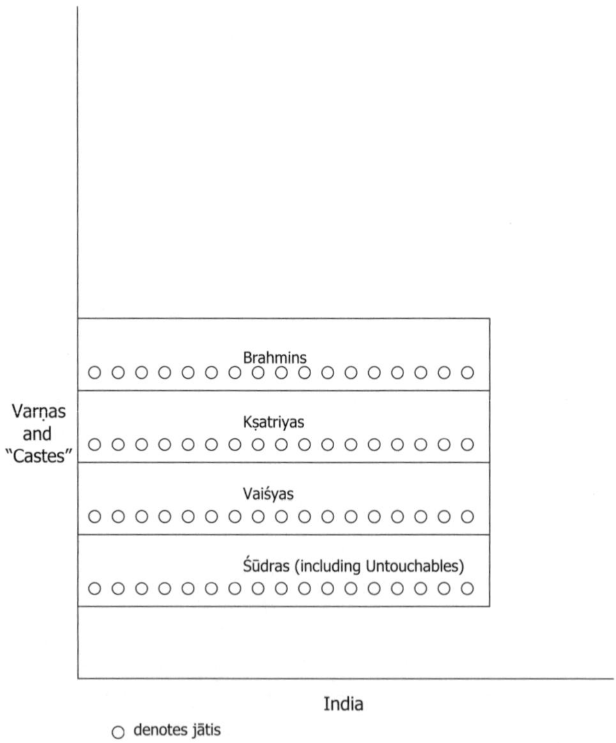

If we now mentally view these two diagrams side by side, we have a base line supporting a number of perpendicular blocks called nations in one diagram, and in the other diagram, we have a number of horizontal bars labeled castes. The blocks in both the diagrams are more or less self-contained units, and their membership is based on birth. In this respect, they are remarkably alike, although an unsubtle view of the matter would propose that a nation must be very different from a caste. In a sense it is, but a remarkable convergence emerges between caste and nation state when their salient features are plotted in this way. In one sense, the difference between them is created by the axis on which they are placed—nation on a vertical axis and caste on the horizontal. The same factor—that both are based on birth, or birth-ascribed—underlies both the axes.

Note how one can be converted into the other by moving the axis. This is the point of the comparison. The ideological compatibility enables one to say that the nation-state is the caste system territorialized; the caste system is the nation-state deterritorialized. That is why one finds layers *upon* layers of castes in India, just as one finds of nations upon nations *alongside* each other in Europe.

An additional consideration suggests that our analysis may be proceeding along the right lines. This consists of the comparability of untouchability and racism. Although the various caste units are distinct, there is free interaction among them in terms of physical proximity—but this is not possible in relation to the untouchables nor is social intercourse possible with them. Thus, as a caste, the untouchables suffer from two disadvantages: social exclusion and limitation of physical movement. In the case of illegal immigrants from a non-Western into a Western country, both these apply—they are kept isolated in camps and excluded both socially and physically from the host society, as currently seen in Australia. An extreme example of this is provided by the blacks in the United States who were allowed *into* the country but *then* socially and physically excluded from white society therein, thereby indicating the common structure (but not etiological links) between racism and untouchability.

I had no idea how my colleagues would react to all of this. Will it be dismissed as an insider's apologetics or taken seriously as a cross-cultural insight? To my pleasant surprise, the response was seen as not only demystifying the caste system but also turning a undeniable negative into a potential positive. This made me think.[8]

* * *

This involvement with human rights in relation to religion, and all the activists and scholars I met in the process, many for the first time, left a profound psychic legacy. It made me realize how thin the dividing line between the sacred and the profane, the religious and the secular, is. It seemed, in a certain sense, somewhat artificial to exclude ideologies from the purview of religion

Thus, while on the one hand my "moral" adventure into human rights began to blur the distinction between the religious and the secular, another enterprise I had voluntarily embarked on began to do the same in relation to the various religions of the world.

A copy of Professor John Hick's book, entitled *A Philosophy of Religion,* fell into my hands when I was teaching in Sydney. It used to be prominently displayed in a book shop I would pass by daily on my way to the office from my nearby apartment. One day, I just bought it. You could say it was a case of familiarity breeding attempt. In any case, having bought it I began to read it. And then mirabile dictu, I began to understand it (or so I thought. Many would doubtless point out that I have never understood it). Only subsequently was I to discover that the book was an academic best seller. (It has gone through four editions, and its Arabic edition has sold over fifty thousand copies.)

While reading it, my mind would wander to comparable concepts or discussions in Hinduism. I thought it might be a good idea to write these up in the form of a book, around the template provided by Professor Hick's book. I did so and sent it to him. He liked it. This led me to wonder if I might carry out the same exercise, this time not in relation to Hinduism but in relation to a school of thought within it, that of Advaita Vedanta. It too was accepted for publication. Nothing succeeds like excess—so I tried the same for Buddhism. This one even got favorable reviews. So, I continued with my project of bringing materials from the Indic religious tradition to the table and turned to Jainism and Sikhism in the same spirit. But the most daring attempt was to try to do the same in relation to the primal religious tradition.

I do not wish to encumber the reader with further bibliograffiti. Actually, it is now beside the point. The various exercises I had undertaken made me realize how humanity has grappled with the same or similar problems in various parts of the world at various times and how little sense it made separating them out into little boxes. John Hick uses the typology of exclusivism, inclusivism, and pluralism to describe the various attitudes religions could have toward each other. Perhaps, the time has come to extend the typology by adding another word to it—universalism.

World's Religions After September 11

It was an event in the realm of international relations, which brought these flashes of insight to a luminous focus, when Al-Qaeda brought down the Twin Towers in New York on September 11, 2001. It illustrated the possibility that political heat can also produce intellectual light. Despite its fabulous speed, the light took some years to appear.

The first reaction was, however, of being scalded by the event.

I remember the event well, like most readers. It is up there, with the Kennedy assassination, when it comes to knowing what I was doing when the news overtook me. I was then in the lounge of the Presbyterian College, diagonally across from the Birks Building, which houses the faculty of religious studies of which I am a member. The lounge abuts on the refectory where I was trying to rustle up a meal for myself. I noticed unusual activity around the TV set. At that moment, a female student broke away from the knot of people around it and passed close by me. As my curiosity got the better of my taciturnity, almost as a languorous afterthought, I asked softly as she went past, "What's happening?"—.

She gently stopped and explained that militants had just ploughed a plane into one of the towers of the World Trade Center in New York, setting it on fire, while another had sliced into the neighboring tower with devastating effect. As she spoke, she moved her fingers ever so lightly, as if spinning some invisible yarn. She was describing a sensational event with a composure that seemed almost superhuman; she spoke in a matter-of-fact way, without any visible or audible sign of panic. Until I realized that I might have mistaken her calmness for indifference, I wondered if Canadians could be that indifferent to what was happening across the border. My first thought, after I had heard what she had to say, seemed incongruous at the time but does not seem so any longer. I heard myself muttering, "So, Gandhi was right after all." This observation piqued the interest of Professor Charles Taylor, when we happened to discuss our reactions some months after the event. My unsurprising explanation of course was that the modern world is so intermeshed that a violent expression of one's grievance was bound to be harmful to a degree out of all proportion to the original offence—so that no matter how deeply one felt oneself to be the victim of an injustice, one was left with *nonviolent* activism as the only viable option to ventilate it. This observation can yield an additional Gandhian nuance with the benefit of hindsight. Rev. Martin Luther King Jr., one of the inheritors of Gandhi's mantle, has famously remarked that "violence is the voice of the unheard." A liberal take on the September 11 events emphasizes the fact that the motivation of the event is perhaps traceable, at least in part, to the unilateral nature of American foreign policy in relation to the Muslim world, a policy thought by many to be alarmingly deaf to what the Muslim world may have to say on certain issues.

That Islam would bear the brunt of negative media attention was obvious to me and to all my colleagues. We once again shared the rueful remark among ourselves that our labors in the study of world religions are truly Sisyphean. For years we try to desensationalize *sati* for instance, by emphasizing its theoretically voluntary nature and its limited incidence. And then, suddenly something happens—like the *sati* of Roop Kunwar in Deorala in 1987—which sends one back to square one. Similarly, I work for decades to disabuse the minds of the students of the grosser misunderstanding of *jihād,* and just when thought I might have succeeded, a 9/11 happens!

But happen it did. And the expected raft of publications—both in the popular media and in academia followed. It soon became apparent, however, that the prejudice against Islam was metastasizing into prejudice against religion in general. All religions now appeared tainted by the same evil brush, in one form or another, in the secular eye. This trend is best epitomized by annexing the title of a book to describe it—*When Religion Becomes Evil.* The following remarks are worth noting in this regard:

> Conflict and security have emerged as particularly urgent arenas in which religion has long been recognized as an important factor. Whether conflict is motivated by religion or aggravated by politicians who exploit religious identities is an ongoing discussion. However, the link itself is unde-

> niable, and is illustrated by all too many recent episodes. Intercommunal violence led to the killing of twenty-one Copts in al-Kosheh in Upper Egypt in January 2000. Horrific bloodshed resulted from the violence between religious groups in Gujarat, India in spring 2002. In autumn 2002 sectarian violence left hundreds dead when violence was unleashed in Nigeria during the attempted hosting of the Miss World beauty contest. The decade of the 1990s witnessed interreligious conflicts in the former Yugoslavia, intercommunal killings in Northern Ireland, and slaughters in Algeria and the Sudan. The potential link between religion and violence has been evidenced in another way by suicides and attacks that have arisen from time to time in connection with unusual new religious movements in the United States, Japan, Switzerland, France, and Belgium.[1]

Religion has virtually become a byword for evil after the events of September 11, 2001. It had already been under assault for some time by the forces of Marxism and feminism as underwriting class discrimination and gender discrimination. The rise of fundamentalism had also added to this sense of religion as something negative in character—raising the specter of violence. Now, with the emergence of terrorism, this hydra-headed monster had begun to belch fire. This realization led me into composing the following item.

> At times like this it is even more important to *feel* clearly than to *think* clearly, for emotions can ignite action in a way thoughts cannot.
>
> The terrorists may have failed to distinguish between devotion and fanaticism, but we cannot fail to distinguish between chastisement and hatred as we react. Crime, diabolically ingenious and parochially perpetrated, must not go unpunished, but the retribution must follow from motives higher than those of revenge. Martin Buber said that nothing becomes a person more than to act toward another in justice—unless it be out of love. To most this Gandhian option will appear pathetic in the incongruity of its sublimity, but the Buberian injunction applies, for to seek revenge is to become unjust in the pursuit of justice.
>
> A disaster on such a scale should at least unsettle our prejudice that terrorism is something out there. What we have witnessed is the globalization of crime by those who

consider the kind of globalization they have witnessed a crime, at least historically. The U.S.A. can no longer live in a safe world of its own so long as the world is not safe. The world will not be safe unless contemporary moral discourse is extended to embrace at least the acknowledgment, if not the righting, of historical wrongs. Is the fact that the tragedy occurred so soon after the near-failure of the racism conference as symbolic of its cause, as the World Trade Center is of its effect? What are a few centuries among friends? Or enemies. Arnold Toynbee once said that Muhammad was Asia's answer to Alexander.

But to understand is not to condone. If the current tragedy does not allow for a resignation of feeling, neither does it allow it to the intellect. While the former sustains a campaign against global terrorism, the latter must find new insight and distinguish between orthodoxy, which is a religious tradition's response to loss of piety and fundamentalism, which is its response to loss of power. Passion then becomes a substitute for power. Passion blinds. Even moral passion blinds. And it becomes possible for some to be blinded by the intensity of the luminosity of their own religious tradition. But perhaps in time heat will produce light.

Will a tragedy of such colossal magnitude not shift our paradigms at least an inch or two?[2]

* * *

People need to be reminded at this juncture that religion is a force for both *good* and *evil*, and to associate it exclusively with evil not only does grave injustice to its history but also forecloses the possibility of harnessing its powers as a force for good.

Here are a few instances that generate the possibility that religion can be a force for good.

(1) At one time the punishment for adultery in the Near East consisted of stoning the woman to death. And, perhaps, such is still the case in some parts of the world. But the following incident should not go unremarked:

An Incident in the Temple

And they went each to his home, and Jesus to the Mount of Olives. At daybreak he appeared again in the temple,

> and all the people gathered round him. He had taken his seat and was engaged in teaching them when the doctors of the law and the Pharisees brought in a woman detected in adultery. Making her stand out in the middle they said to him, "Master, this woman was caught in the very act of adultery. In the Law Moses has laid down that such women are to be stoned. What do you say about it?" They put the question as a test, hoping to frame a charge against him.
>
> Jesus bent down and wrote with his finger on the ground. When they continued to press their question he sat up straight and said, "That one of you who is faultless shall throw the first stone." Then once again he bent down and wrote on the ground.
>
> When they heard what he said, one by one they went away, the eldest first, and Jesus was left alone, with the woman still standing there. Jesus again sat up and said to the woman, "Where are they? Has no one condemned you?"
>
> "No one, sir," she said.
>
> Jesus replied, "No more do I. You may go; do not sin again."
>
> (Gospel according to John 7:53-8: 11; *New English Bible*)[3]

(2) Here, we see religion reshaping social morality in a humane way. An example from Islam is provided by the life of the Prophet, which sets the norm for Muslims. It encourages a pattern for egalitarianism in human relations.

> Once the Prophet asked his companions to prepare goat's meat for the group as they were traveling. One said he would kill the goat; another said he would skin it; another volunteered to cook it. The Prophet said he would gather the wood for the fire. His companions immediately protested: "You are God's Messenger. We will do everything." "I know you would," said the Prophet, "but that would be discrimination. God does not want his servants to behave as if they were superior to their companions."[4]

(3) The following evidence from Japanese Buddhism would serve to make the same point—that religion can be a force for good:

Publishing the Sutras

> Tetsugen, a devotee of Zen in Japan, decided to publish the sutras, which at that time were available only in Chinese. The books were to be printed with wood blocks in an edition of seven thousand copies, a tremendous undertaking.
>
> Tetsugen began by traveling and collecting donations for this purpose. A few sympathizers would give him a hundred pieces of gold, but most of the time the received only small coins. He thanked each donor with equal gratitude. After ten years Tetsugen had enough to begin his task.
>
> It happened that at that time the Uji River overflowed. Famine followed. Tetsugen took the funds he had collected for the books and spent them to save others from starvation. Then he began again his work of collecting.
>
> Several years afterwards an epidemic spread over the country. Tetsugen again gave away what he had collected, to help his people.
>
> For a third time he started his work, and after twenty years his wish was fulfilled. The printing blocks which produced the first edition of sutras can be seen today in the Obaku monastery in Kyoto.
>
> The Japanese tell their children that Tetsugen made three sets of sutras, and that the first two invisible sets surpass even the last.[5]

(4) The way the Truth and Reconciliation Commission in South Africa helped resolve the problematic legacy of apartheid provides another example of how religion can be a force for good. The following account is worth noting here:

> In Edmonton, Archbishop Tutu told a story of four men who had murdered young people in a small town. They appeared before his commission in the same town in a crowded hall before the very people whose relatives had been lost. They admitted their guilt. They expressed their remorse. They asked for forgiveness.
>
> It was a hot night. The hall had been filled with anger and passion. After some moments of silence, the crowd broke into applause and the guilty men wept. God was in the room that night, said Archbishop Tutu.[6]

(5) The Holocaust provides an example of what happens when religion goes bad, but the following reaction to the Holocaust also illustrates how religion can be a force for good. There now exists

> Tzedaka, a faith-based foundation funded by German Christians seeking to help heal the wounds inflicted by the Nazis. Tzedaka's projects include Beit Eliezer, a 24-bed nursing home for Holocaust survivors in northern Israel, and an inn in Shravei Tzion, where survivors can have free 10-day vacations. . . .
>
> Tzedaka, Hebrew for "charity," opened its first resort in Israel in 1960, in the northern town of Nahariya, said Yohanan Beyer, 64, the group's top administrator. . . .
>
> Lachs Etelka, 77, an Auschwitz survivor, has a blue death-camp tattoo—A-16067—burned into her left arm and is still haunted by memories, for instance of trying to drink urine to quench an impossible thirst.
>
> "I still see pictures in my head and I wake up at night," she said.
>
> During her first day at the Tzedak Inn in the northern Israeli town of Shavei Tzion, she was stunned to be welcomed so warmly by Germans.
>
> "The way they greeted me—I have no words. In every sea there are many types of fish."[7]

(6) How religion tended to act as a brake on blind vengeance even in biblical times may be deduced from the following passage:

> An earlier historical example of creative interplay between nature and morality is the biblical command to build cities of refuge for the accidental killer. The authors of the Bible certainly understood the inherent human impulse for vengeance. In one of the most subtle and innovative chapters of the Bible, God commands Moses to "appoint . . . cities of refuge . . . that the manslayer who killed any person by accident may flee into." Willful murderers were not entitled to such refuge from the "blood revenge," but accidental killers were entitled to protection until passions cooled. The Bible recognized that the passion for revenge may be just as great against the accidental killer as against the premeditated murderer. To the dead victim's family, there

> may be little difference. Their loved one is dead, and the person who caused his death is guilty and deserves to die. The writers of the Bible understood this human reality, but they also insisted that to understand is not necessarily to justify. The Bible seeks to protect the less culpable killer from the understandable passions of the blood avenger by allowing the killer to seek refuge in a designated place for a specified period of time.[8]

(7) On December 1, 1955, Rosa Parks, a black woman in Montgomery, Alabama, decided she would not give up her seat to a white passenger and was arrested for her act of courage or defiance. Her arrest triggered a boycott of buses in Montgomery by the blacks, who refused to ride the buses unless the laws were changed. The black churches, under the leadership of Martin Luther King, Jr., joined the boycott. The boycott, which lasted for 381 days, almost bankrupted the bus company. On Nov. 13, 1956 the U.S. Supreme Court ruled in favor of ending segregation in the buses, declaring it unconstitutional.

"But the boycott continued for about a month more. Dr. King and other black leaders would not agree to end the boycott until the city actually started obeying the law and ended the segregation."[9] Dr. King ultimately paid for his courageous intervention with his life, but not before he had been to the mountain top and seen the promised land.

(8) Nor must the interaction between religion and society be necessarily viewed as a one-way street, when two-way traffic is possible. Mary Robinson spoke these memorable words at the Oslo Conference on Freedom of Religion or Belief, which met from August 12 to August 15, 1998:

> The major religions, while concerned with ultimate questions, frequently present themselves as protectors and promoters of human dignity. They see themselves in particular as the defenders of the deprived, the poor, the discriminated against. So their religious freedom is a freedom in society not merely to believe and to worship but also to uphold the cause of the deprived. In these circumstances they must ensure that their own internal practices are not discriminatory on grounds of gender or race or class. They have to learn from the good practice of wider society as well as teach it.[10]

* * *

But how does one bring this fact to public attention—that religion is a force in human affairs capable of being harnessed both for good or evil? It was in wrestling with this that I had not quite a eureka or even an aha experience but perhaps what would qualify as a light bulb experience. Perhaps, one could hold a global congress to highlight this possibility. Such a congress could also be used to further the project of moving toward a Universal Declaration of Human Rights by the Worlds' Religions. While this idea was gestating, I learned that the Iranian human rights activist, Madam Shirin Ebadi, had been awarded the Nobel Peace Prize for 2003. Then I learned she was about to visit Toronto! I had to miss out on my presentation at the Roundtable on Indology in Cambridge, Massachusetts, to fly out to try to see her. I did succeed in seeing her and in presenting my ideas to her. What would be more corrective of popular misconceptions, about Islam in particular and religion in general, if a Muslim woman released the draft of the proposed Universal Declaration of Human Rights by the World's Religions?

Through an interpreter, Madam Ebadi asked me sharply on which side would I stand if religion came in conflict with human rights. "Human rights," I said without hesitation. Religions for me are intended as a humanizing force in the world. She promised to consider the request.

Weeks passed into months, and yet there was no word from her. And preparations for a congress in 2006 were now afoot. Just when I did not know what to do, I happened to browse through the local paper, which contained the curious bit of information that one of her daughters was a student at McGill. I activated an Iranian connection I had and soon, somewhat improbably, I had her daughter's phone number in my hands. Incredulously I dialed it. It was answered by a female voice, which indeed turned out to be that of Madam Ebadi's daughter. Even more amazingly, although I was the petitioner, she offered to come and see me. I explained my predicament to her.

Two days later, I received an email confirming Madam Ebadi's participation in the Congress. In addition to His Holiness the Dalai Lama, Archbishop Desmond Tutu, Bishop Carlos Belo of Timor Leste, and noted author and human-rights advocate, Elie Wiesel, she also graciously agreed to be a patron of the project dedicated to formulating a Universal Declaration of Human Rights by the World's Religions, This was the second encouraging sign that I might after all be on the right track. The first major sign had come earlier, when I first thought up the idea that a global congress on world religions after September 11 seemed called for.

"It seems a good idea to you," I said to myself, "But you need a reality check." What should that be? It occurred to me that I should first go and invite Professor Huston Smith to the Congress. If he accepted the invitation, then I should proceed with the idea, otherwise let go of it.

I met Huston Smith in Berkeley at his home, shared my idea with him, and invited him to the Congress. He paused briefly and then said, "I am eighty-two now. I don't know whether I will be around then or in a condition to attend even if I am around. But the project is important enough for me to say that, if I am around and in good health, I shall come."

It was a decisive moment. The die had been cast.

Professor Huston Smith, to the cheerful and grateful satisfaction of all of us, did attend the Congress. But not without some drama.

With four days to go for the Congress, I came to my office and was greeted by a taped message. It was from Mrs. Smith. She was concerned about Huston's forthcoming visit because on a recent occasion he had to be taken to the emergency room while attending another conference, and she wasn't sure if the doctors would let him come to Montreal. She, therefore, advised me to make contingent plans just in case (which of course we had).

All that we could do was to wait. At the appointed time, however, Huston arrived—in a wheel chair, no doubt, but very much here.

I could not resist the temptation, when we met, of asking him if he had discussed the visit with his wife. "Yes," he said, "she asked me why I wanted to go to Montreal. I said, 'To see you.' She nodded. And I am here now."

It is difficult not to feel overwhelmed at such moments and to think that, perhaps, such moments are really what life is all about.

The questions that were put to him on September 13, 2006, when he spoke on the theme of religion and science, might be of interest:

> (1) Your model of concentric circles suggests that science should be a subset of religion, but do they really overlap in the questions they seek to answer?
>
> Doesn't science answer what, where, when, and how, while religion answers the why?

(2) What is the best scientific hope for Intelligent Design?—DNA, consciousness, or . . . ?

(3) I was asked to answer a question that I have no answer to because I find it clear and evident for myself: Why do I need to believe? Please help me answer.

(4) In this age, the polarity of science and religion seems to be moving toward an absorption of religion by science. That is, science is now being called a religion in and of itself. Is science as a religion any less valuable than traditional religion?

(5) As a historian of religion, could you please comment briefly on the ways different religions of the world (or major spokespersons of these religions?) relate to science?

(6) If you had to summarize your thesis about "why religion matters," what would you say?

(7) How old are you?

(8) Do you believe God is supreme intelligence?[11]

I am getting a little ahead of the story now. So, to revert to the master narrative: with Huston Smith's willing acceptance of participation in the Congress, the *idea* of holding a congress became a viable one. The question of moving from the idea to a *concept* still remained a pressing one.

For this to happen, two requirements, which were interrelated, had to be met. Who was to run the congress and how was one to secure the funding? The two were interconnected in the sense that, if we has a professional conference organizer (PCO), it could help raise the funds. Or else, if we had the funds, we could hire a PCO. The situation had the makings of a chicken-and-egg problem: Which comes first? The interesting aspect of the issue is that, while it may be a conundrum from a theoretical point of view, from a practical point of view each of the two horns of the dilemma can become a peg to hang a solution on. (If one needs to make an omelette, then if one has the chicken, one can get it to lay an egg—or if one has the egg, then one can proceed straightway to the omelette.)

So, I decided to seek out a PCO first and, to this end, circulated and advertised a proposal with a view to get a PCO interested in the project.

The proposal, surprisingly, attracted four responses. I made it clear to each party that the firm which helped raise the money would get the contract.

This stringent condition ultimately left only one contender in the field!

I had, in acting the way I did, followed the advice offered by Parkinson,[12] without being conscious of it. Parkinson has argued, largely tongue-in-cheek, but not entirely, that the ideal advertisement was one which elicited only one response, and that would be the right response. He illustrated his point with the help of an ad designed to identify the prime minister for a country, which he designed and then asserted that only one person would apply for the job and the person would be the right person for the job. For the sake of argument, he did admit the possibility that more than one person may apply for the job. Say two. What was one to do then?

Parkinson's answer is simplicity itself. He recommends that the secretary (presumably female) should be asked to choose between the two. This might sound preposterous, he admits. But he also adds that this amounts to taking a rather shallow view of the situation, because all that he has done is factor in another variable into the equation, namely, the sex appeal of the candidate.

My method, though not as glamorous, had produced an outcome that would have been relished by him—that only one party eventually applied—after I had applied the stringent condition, and that it was the right one.

This felicitous outcome, however, came with a price tag. The PCO had succeeded in obtaining a line of credit for the Congress from an agency, but before the agency would extend it, it insisted that the Congress be accepted as a post-Parliament event by the Council for a Parliament of World's Religions (CPWR). This body had organized three prestigious parliaments of religions in quinquennial succession: at Chicago (1993), Cape Town (1999), and Barcelona (2004) and had expressed an interest in according the status of a post-Parliament event to the global congress planned for Montreal in 2006.

The application with the funding agency had been filed, and the arrangements went down to the wire. We just couldn't get the CPWR to respond, and I finally received word that doomsday had arrived. If we did not have CPWR's approval by a certain day, the funding agency would not consider our application.

I came into the office that morning—not knowing what to expect, and not knowing what to do—when it happened. I opened the email and lo and behold—the entire document was there, meeting to a T the requirements of the funding agency. I resisted as best as I could the temptation to see the invisible hand (of God or Adam Smith I am not quite sure) in all this, as if confirming the whole enterprise at an altogether different level.

Another incident bearing on the formative phase of the Congress bears recounting. It has to do with the draft of the Universal Declaration of Human Rights by the World's Religions, which was showcased at this congress and was formally unveiled for public discussion on September 12, 2006 by Madam Shirin Ebadi. At the time about which I am writing, this proposed declaration was merely an idea, an idea whose time perhaps had not come, considering the lukewarm response the proposal originally elicited,(when it was mentioned as one of the ways in which the legacy of the Project on Religion and Human Rights could extend into the future, once that project itself had run its course in the mid-1990s). Such was my frame of mind when I visited Boston during this period and went out for lunch with Virginia Strauss, who directed the Boston Research Center of the Soka Gakkai International in Cambridge, Massachusetts. As we wound up our meal and discussion, I remember telling her despondently that perhaps I should let go of the idea. At which she quietly asked, in a matter-of-fact way, which was almost prosaic, "What could we do to help?"

I still remember my reaction to her words because my own reaction so astonished me. As I heard her say what she did, I unaccountably but palpably shed my despondency and felt reinvigorated to pursue the idea further. Sometimes, the applause of even one person can go a long way, and sometimes it does not even have to be applause, just a nod of approval. Sometimes, not even that, and a mere implicit expression of confidence—direct or indirect—suffices. Kipling may well have been right when he identified words as the most potent drug invented by human beings. Because I believed that she had doubtless forgotten all about it, I gratefully reminded her of that earlier meeting in the same restaurant, almost a decade after she had uttered the magic words. To my considerable surprise, she said that, on the contrary, she remembered the occasion well. I still find it hard to believe that six simple words could turn around one's mood so completely, as if a mathematician were to change the minus sign into a plus sign with a casual stroke of the chalk on a black board. Had it not happened to me, I would have a hard time believing today that such an instantaneous transformation was possible.

* * *

Two nights before the Congress, a well-meaning colleague came into my office and berated me, "Do you realize what a high risk adventure you have embarked on? Who is going to come to the Congress in these days of terrorism? What if no one turned up like in the John Lennon song, which says, 'What if someone declared war but nobody came?' And what are they going to eat? There are no places to eat at the convention center nor near it."

When I went to bed that day, I had nightmares of no-show delegates starving to death, in the halls of the convention center, as a result of not eating at nonexistent restaurants.

* * *

The fears of my colleague were, however, not totally unfounded. A shooting incident overtook us right in the middle of the Congress, and its coverage made the Congress disappear from the media. So, the Congress took a few bullets too.

Dr. Shanta Srivastava was to teach a course at Dawson College on September 13, but she decided to give her class a break in order to attend the Congress. While at the Congress, she received a frantic phone call from her daughter about her well-being, because a shooting incident had been reported at Dawson College, in the course of which one female student died and others were injured by a lone gunman, Kimveer Gill, age twenty-five, who had gone on a shooting spree.

It slowly came to light that Kimveer Gill had shot one person dead and wounded several before turning the gun on himself. The police was later to discover a notepad in his car containing hand-drawn sketches of routes leading to four schools: Université de Montréal, Vanier College, a Laval High School, and Dawson College. On the page with directions to Université de Montréal, Kimveer Gill had scribbled the words, "too big." No one quite knows why he chose Dawson College, but they feel that he was trying to replicate the 1999 Columbine High School massacre in Colorado, where thirteen students died at the hands of two armed students.[13]

Police initially thought that they had a terrorist attack on their hands, which fortunately was not the case. Otherwise, the Congress would have been hoisted by its own petard!

An explanation of the incident was sought at the daily press conference of the Congress. The issue was particularly poignant for us, as it had occurred right in the middle of a congress which focused on September 11. Deepak Chopra addressed the Congress that morning, and he remarked during the press conference, "I am curious to know what is [Kimveer Gill's] story, what has he been telling himself? And what's his part in our collective story?" Others saw in it the futility of the secular denial of the religious dimension of life, which often leaves young people without a spiritual anchor.

The simultaneity of the Congress on the one hand and of the fear of terrorism, which the incident evoked right in its midst, on the other, gave an existential flavor to the dilemma articulated in the following remarks:

> Far from withering away, then, religion has assumed new salience. But this has stirred new anxieties. The "ambivalence of the sacred"—the fact that religion spawns both good and evil—has led on the one hand to a global resurgence of religion and on the other to global pressures to mitigate religious hazards. This in turn has given new urgency to questions of how to structure the freedom of religion or belief. In our pluralistic world, the alternatives are stark. Either we must find ways for groups with differing beliefs to live together (which appears to be possible only by respecting freedom of religion or belief, whether through state-enforced protections or through internalizing norms of respect for the dignity and religious choices of others), or we must face constant friction, all too frequent warfare, and the ultimate risk of nuclear Armageddon.[14]

* * *

Several months had passed since the Congress had met at Palais des Congrès in Montreal from September 11 to 15 under the banner, World's Religions After September 11—A Global Congress. I had recently returned from India and was about to unlock the door to my office, when I saw what looked like a familiar face peering in my direction. I had scarcely time to wonder if she was a student from my Study of World Religions class last fall, when she asked whether I had time to see her.

It turned out that, in the present climate of opinion, she was having difficulty defending Islam among people she knew. I reminded her that some of the points she was raising had been dealt with by Huston Smith. As I fumbled for the pages in his book, she said, "O Huston Smith. I met him when he came to the Congress, I even asked him a question."

"You did?" I looked up.

"Yes. It was right after the session was over. He was sitting at the table on the stage. You may remember that he was taking questions in writing. I went up to him and handed him a note which read, *'Please write me something true.'* "

"What did he say?" My heart stood still with pedagogical pride.

"He cast a knowing look at me through the corners of his eyes, and a grandfatherly smile flicked across his face. 'That is very good,' he said and then he wrote, *'Absolute perfection reigns, and it is our job to conform our lives to that fact.'* "

That note was now a prized possession of hers.

We exchanged glances of deep mutual understanding.

No congress could be considered worthless if it had succeeded in spiritually stirring the soul of a single student.[15]

Conclusion

This book may now be brought to a conclusion.

Even as I roamed the world of the comparative study of religion with its many wonders, I always remained linked to my own Hindu tradition on account of regularly teaching courses in it. The two experiences seemed complementary, and occasionally I even wondered if they were two, for I would draw on one—or even on the secular realm—to clarify some point of the other. For instance, I would draw on American political experience to explain a quintessentially Hindu distinction between *nirguṇa* and *saguṇa brahman* to mostly Canadian students. This debate within Hinduism as to whether God is ultimately impersonal or personal, whether the ultimate is ultimately without attributes or with attributes, resonates throughout the history of Hinduism, and echoes of it can be heard in the other religious traditions as well. The tradition of Kabala in Judaism, which speaks of En Sof rather than Yahweh, is said to offer a parallel from medieval times, and the Paul Tillich's distinction between Godhead and God offers one in modern times.

The distinction is so central to philosophical Hinduism that, whereas in the case of these other traditions it can be a footnote, or an endnote, in the study of Hinduism it is more like a headline. After struggling to put it within the reach of the students in various conventional ways, an exercise in unconventional wisdom proved far more fruitful. I would ask the class the seemingly irrelevant question: how many of you have seen Mount Rushmore? Invariably a few hands would go up, and apparently almost all would have heard of it. Now what, you might ask, could the faces of the four great presidents of the United States—George Washington, Thomas Jefferson, Theodore Roosevelt and Abraham Lincoln—carved out on the side of a mountain in the Black Hills of South Dakota, have to do with the distinction between *nirguṇa brahman* and *saguṇa brahman* in Hinduism?

I would ask the class to visualize the side of the mountain, which had these figures, and compare it in their imagination with the side that did not have them—the other side that was plain and bare. Well then, the side with the four faces had the distinguishing attributes consisting of the four faces, which the other side did not possess. Thus, one side of the mountain could be called *saguṇa*, with distinguishing attributes, and the other side was *nirguṇa*, without distinguishing attributes. After the students got over the element of surprise involved in the comparison, they would often get the point that then paved the way for making the profounder point that both *nirguṇa* and *saguṇa* are aspects of the same *brahman*—just as both the sides, with and without the representations of the presidential faces, belonged to the *same* mountain.

I would of course use the two terms—*nirguṇa* and *saguṇa brahman*—without prioritizing them (in a lapse from prejudice for someone who formally teaches courses in Advaita Vedānta which favors the former) to emphasize the ongoing nature of the debate. And as to why the debate might be an ongoing one was also best indicated by a further secular example. I would ask the class, "which of the two they considered above the other in significance: the *president* of the United States, or the *presidency* of the United States?" There can of course be no presidency without the president and no president without the presidency. In the former case, presidency would be a mere abstraction without the president, while in the latter case, it would not be possible to call someone a president in the absence of the institution of the presidency. But to which of the two would one accord primacy? Often the difficulty the class experienced in answering the question helped it get the point as to why the difference between *nirguṇa* and *saguṇa* was such a debated topic in Hinduism. It, of course, had to be clarified that to say the *brahman* was without characteristics did not imply that it was characterless,[1] or to say that it was featureless did not imply that it was a substance bereft of attributes but rather that it transcended the distinction between substance and attribute.[2]

Sometimes this last statement caused epistemic consternation, which again was set to rest with a secular example. I pointed out that all material objects possessed certain dimensions, such as length, width, height, and so on (as, for example, the chair one is sitting on, or the book one is reading while sitting in the chair). Thus, a chair could be said to be on object, a substance, which possessed certain attributes. Space, however, is not a thing or substance; it *is*, but it does not possess the attributes of a substance such as length, width, or height. Thus, it transcends the distinction between substance and attribute. The fact, however, that it does not possess any material attribute in this sense and is immaterial in nature does not mean that it does not exist. Rather, it turns out to be the case that material objects exist in immaterial space! In such ways, the students were able to perhaps grasp what was meant when it was claimed that *nirguṇa brahman* was beyond any empirical attributes.

The fact that the study of religion was advanced by secular examples did not, of course, mean that the subject of study ceased to be sacred. But even at its most sacred, sometimes the secular came in handy, to the point of verging on the risqué. At the end of a course on world religions, I was sometimes asked to specify the religion I belonged to. This was of course a great compliment, but I wasn't sure to whom—to me or to the textbook (which was none other than Huston Smith's *The World's Religions*, a book so evenhanded yet sympathetic in its treatment of the various religions of the world that the followers of each religion would like to count Huston Smith among their own). At this point, I would share the following observation with the class. "Let me try to answer your question in the following way. You have doubtless heard of Doris Day—the American actress who symbolized the girl next door. She once came on a TV program and remarked, "What can I say? I have a six year old daughter and people still think I am a virgin!" Similarly, I have been teaching comparative religion for twenty years now, and people still think I am a Hindu!"

Some other questions required defter moves, like the one which would be sometimes put to me after I had unfolded the landscape of the Hindu worldview on the blackboard: "Do you believe in all this?"

The best answer I came up was the one Professor Harvey Cox reminded me of when I was fumbling on one such occasion: "If I say that I live in a haunted house, then does it mean that I believe in ghosts?"

These pedagogical adventures made academic life appear seamless, as I lectured on Hinduism and World Religions, and began writing on religion and human rights, and specially on religions as a positive resource for human rights.

Participation in this discourse set me on a trajectory that brought the light of analytical differentiation to the inchoate existential unity of my professional life. For, as a result of pursuing the relationship of religion and human rights, I was forced to look at, first, the relationship of Hinduism to the realm of the human rights discourse,[3] and then to its relation to religion in general as well.[4] It also produced a third consequence: the need to face the divide between the religious and the secular.

These background developments brought the events of September 11, 2001 into a sharper focus and gave rise to three considerations, which ultimately led to the convening of a global congress on World's Religions After September 11. The first was the realization that the events of September 11 had turned religion into a bad word. The word had acquired a negative connotation. And it was not just Islam but religion per se that had come under a cloud. This could only be considered unfortunate, as religion is a force in human affairs and, like any force, could be harnessed for good or evil. (Fire can cook one's meal and also burn down one's house. Electricity can warm one's house or electrocute one.) If religion was viewed only negatively, then it meant shutting it out as a possible source of promoting human flourishing. No doubt, much evil has been perpetrated in the name of religion, but much good has also come out of it. It was Christianity that put an end to the gory gladiatorial contests in Rome, and it was the advent of Islam, which put an end to female infanticide in Arabia. It seemed shortsighted to prematurely shut it out as a source of human good. The medieval world saw the hand of God in everything. The modern world sees his fingerprints everywhere, inasmuch as it blames religion for the ills of our time. But facts indicate that this is a half-truth, and we would be holding on to the wrong half if we looked upon religion only as a source of evil. Now that we know that attempts to suppress human religiosity are no more likely to succeed than attempts to repress human sexuality, the mantra of the Congress was that, if religion is part of the problem, it had to be part of the solution.

But before religion can become a part of the solution, one had to understand the nature of religious fanaticism. Fanaticism results from standing so close to one's religious tradition as to be blinded by the intensity of its luminosity, instead of seeing the whole world transfigured in its light. In the same vein, orthodoxy is the response of a religious tradition to its perceived loss of *piety* in the public square, while fundamentalism is the response of a religious tradition to its perceived loss of *power* in the public square and embodies a kind of nostalgia for the future. The ingredients underlying fanaticism, fundamentalism, and orthodoxy, however, contain a positive element—the search for commitment in the case of fanaticism, the search for sanctity in the case of orthodoxy, and the search for identity in the case of fundamentalism. It becomes important to distil their essences in such a way that religion becomes a plus rather than a minus sign in the equation of humanity's well-being.

The second consideration arose out of growing familiarity with the human rights discourse. The Universal Declaration of Human Rights was adopted by the U.N. on December 10, 1948, still celebrated as Human Rights Day around the world. It was, however, adopted after the Second World War, which ended in 1945. The Second World War, however, could be looked upon as the outcome of the forces unleashed by *secular* extremism, which is how the movements of fascism, totalitarianism, communism, and imperialism could be characterized. The Universal Declaration of Human Rights was adopted by the world after these forces had run their course. It is now widely believed that *religious* extremism is on the rise. Should we not learn from history and try to get a Universal Declaration of Human Rights by the World's Religions in place before the situation gets out of hand? One need not labor under the illusion that this measure alone will stem the tide of religious extremism; however, one might consider the possibility that it might abate it somewhat or at least mitigate its worst excesses. It would be harder for religions to violate norms they have themselves accepted by coming together of their own free will, than if there was no such document in existence.

The third consideration was suggested by a reflection on contemporary history. Ever since the rise of the modern West, intellectual life in the West and the rest of the world, which came under its influence, had been governed by what may be called the "secular hypothesis." This was the view that as nations progressed politically, economically, and socially, religion would either disappear together (as in some versions of Marxism) or would at least disappear from public life and become a purely private affair (according to mainline Western liberal thought). The secular hypothesis implied that Europe's past was the world's future and remained unchallenged until 1979—the year of the Iranian Revolution. Everything seemed to be going according to plan until then. The Iranian Revolution, however, signaled the reentry of religion in public life with a vengeance. This development could be dismissed as an aberration but not for long because the level of fundamentalism has since been rising steadily in all the religions of the world—Hinduism and Buddhism, which may have considered themselves immune to it, not excepted. A host of events since then, associated mostly but not solely with Islam, such as the Salman Rushdie affair, the advocacy of the shariah by immigrant Muslim communities in Europe, the murder of Theo van Gogh, the cartoon affair, the textbook controversy in California about the depiction of Hinduism, the furor around the remarks citied by Pope Benedict XVI while speaking at Regensburg University in Germany—all seem to suggest that the religious and secular realms may be negotiating the terms of the reentry of religion in the public sphere without being quite aware of it. The release of the draft of a Universal Declaration of Human Rights by the World's Religions at the global congress could then be seen as an attempt to negotiate the terms of this reentry in a more congenial fashion. This is important because religion can no longer be dismissed as a bad dream, which will go away, and is likely to become a recurring nightmare if it is not accorded its rightful place in the public square.

I would like to conclude with two important insights provoked by the Congress, which, like all great insights, appear obvious in hindsight. But their obviousness should not blind us to their potential in transforming how we view religion and the way we study it.

The first was that religions are a force of evil when they work against each other and a force for good when they work together. Attempts on the part of one religion to convert members of another religion is an obvious example of religions working against each other. When religions fear that people are trying to steal the flock, they come in conflict and become a force for evil. However, when religions come together to alleviate suffering, they become a force for good. When the actions of religions center on apparently "secular" causes such as healthcare or the spread of literacy, religions can apparently even be brought together by secularism. This seems to be the deeper message of the following anecdote: When Guru Nanak (1469–1583), the founder of Sikhism, proposed the building of mosques, the Hindus objected, and when he proposed the building of temples, the Muslims objected—so he asked both the communities to join in building bathrooms that could be used by all human beings irrespective of their religious background.

The second insight was the distinction between a "marked" and an "unmarked" human being, which is overlooked in human rights discourse to its detriment. As a member of a nation-state or as a citizen, I am a marked human being, but when viewed merely as a human being unrelated to a state, I am an unmarked human being. It is worth noting that all of us can be placed in either of these frames. Let us now apply this to the study of religion. If then, as a Hindu (marked), I am a legatee of the Hindu religious tradition (and as a

Christian of the Christian, and so on), then what is my inheritance as a human being (unmarked)? As a Muslim, I may be heir to the Islamic tradition, but one is a human being all the time, even as one is a Hindu, a Christian, or a Muslim. What, then, is my legacy as a *human being*? If, as a Hindu, I inherit the Hindu religious tradition, then, do I not, as a human being, inherit the entire religious tradition of humanity?

Notes

Banaras

1. Paraphrased from Aṅguttara-Nikāya, as cited in Walpola Rahula, *What the Buddha Taught* (New York: Grove Press Inc, 1974), 27.

2. Ananda A. Coomaraswamy and Sister Nivedita, *Myths of the Hindus & the Buddhists* (New York: Dover Publications, Inc., 1967) 252–55.

Nainital

1. See *Talks with Ramana Maharshi* (Tiruvannamalai, India: Sri Ramanasraman, 1984), 442. Paraphrased. See also 305 and 334.

2. *The Complete Works of Sister Nivedita*. Birth Centenary Volume. (Calcutta: Ramakrishna Sarada Mission, 1967), 286–88.

Fatehpur

1. P.V. Kane, *History of Dharmaśāstra* (Poona: Bhandarkar Oriental Research Institute, 1974) Vol. V, Part I, 650.

2. Ainslie T. Embree, ed., *The Hindu Tradition* (New York: Random House, 1972), 258. Diacritics removed.

Delhi

1. Kirin Narayan, *Storytellers, Saints and Scoundrels: Folk Narratives in Hindu Religious Teaching* (Delhi: Motilal Banardidass, 1992), 161–67. The words in the brackets are the storyteller's.

The Hindu World

1. S. Radhakrishnan, *The Principal Upaniṣads* (Atlantic Highlands, N.J.: Humanities Press, 1978 [1953]), 594.

2. Joe and Guinevere Miller, *The Spiritual Teaching of Ramana Maharshi* (Boston & London: Shambhala, 1988), 74–75.

3. Heinrich Zimmer, *Myths and Symbols in Indian Art and Civilization* (New York and Evanston: Harper & Row, 1962), 32–33; emphasis added.

4. J. Mackenzie, *Hindu Ethics: A Historical and Critical Essay* (London: Oxford University Press, 1922).

5. P.V. Kane, *History of Dharmaśāstra*, 2nd ed. (Poona: Bhandarkar Oriental Research Institute, 1977) Vol. V, Part II, 1627.

6. S. Cromwell Crawford, *Dilemmas of Life and Death: Hindu Ethics in a North American Context* (Albany, N.Y.: State University of New York Press, 1995), 5.

7. Apparently others have made the connection too. See T.M.P Mahadevan, *Outlines of Hinduism* (Bombay: Chetana, 1971), 62.

8. Some modern scholars have also invoked this sonnet in their discussion of Hinduism; see S. Cromwell Crawford, *Dilemmas of Life and Death*, 202.

9. Robert Frost, "Stopping by the Woods on a Snowy Evening," in Edward Connery Lathem, ed., *The Poetry of Robert Frost* (New York: Holt, Rinehart and Winston, 1979), 224.

The Hinjew Connection

1. Cited in D.S. Sarma, *Hinduism Through the Ages* (Bombay: Bharatiya Vidya Bhavan, 1956), 90.

2. Ibid, 91; emphasis added.

3. Cited in David S. Noss and John B. Noss, *A History of the World's Religions*, 9th ed. (Upper Saddle River, N.J.: Prentice Hall, 1994), 441.

4. K.M. Panikkar, *Hindu Society at Cross Roads* (Bombay: Asia Publishing House, 1961), 117.

5. Swami Vivekananda, *The Complete Works of Swami Vivekananda*. Mayavati Memorial Edition (Calcutta: Advaita Ashrama, 1979) Vol. V, 233. It must be pointed out that, whether a holocaust of this kind occurred or not, remains to be established objectively; such a perception, however, sometimes appears in the writings of spokespersons of Hinduism, and often in the literature produced by the Hindu right.

6. See Ainslie T. Embree, ed., *Sources of Indian Tradition*, 2nd ed. (New York: Columbia University Press, 1988) Vol. I, 508.

7. R.C. Majumdar, ed., *The Moghul Empire* (Bombay: Bharatiya Vidya Bhavan, 1974), 306–307.

8. Mohandas K. Gandhi, *An Autobiography: The Story of My Experiments with Truth* (Boston: Beacon Press, 1993), 35.

9. Ruth R. Wisse, *If I Am Not For Myself: The Liberal Betrayal of the Jews* (New York: The Free Press, 1992), 18–19.

10. Ibid, 187.

11. Ibid, 81.

12. Ibid, 179.

13. Ibid, 137.

14. Ibid, 171.

15. Ibid, 167.

16. Ibid, 163.

Experiencing Christianity

1. Cited in Anantanand Rambachan, "Hindu-Christian Consultation: Towards One World Family," *Current Dialogue* (December 1997): 31.

2. Wilfred Owen, "Parable of the Old Man and the Young," in Siegfreid Sassoon, ed., *Poems* (London: Chatto & Windus, 1920), 9.

3. R. Tagore, *Gitanjali* (Boston: International Pocket Library, 1912), 57.

4. R.C. Majumdar, ed., *The Vedic Age* (London: George Allen & Unwin Ltd., 1952), 365.

5. R.C. Zaehner, trans., *Hindu Scriptures* (London: J.M. Dent & Sons Ltd., 1966), 4.

6. Vettam Mani, *Puranic Encyclopedia* (Delhi: Motilal Banarsidass, 1974), 873.

7. John McCrae, "In Flanders Fields," in *In Flanders Fields and Other Poems* (London: Holder and Stoughton, 1919), 15.

8. Mohandas K. Gandhi, *An Autobiography: The Story of My Experiments with Truth* (Boston: Beacon Press, 1993), 33–34.

9. Krister Stendahl, "From God's Perspective We Are All Minorities," *The Journal of Religious Pluralism* II (1992), 3.

10. Ibid, 5.

11. Willard G. Oxtoby, ed., *World Religions: Western Traditions* (Toronto: Oxford University Press, 1996), 199.

Teaching Islam

1. Eric J. Sharpe, "Study of Religion: Methodological Issues," in Mircea Eliade, editor-in-chief, *The Encyclopedia of Religion* (New York: The Macmillan Company, 1987) Vol. 14, 85.

2. See Percival Spear, *India: A Modern History* (Ann Arbor: The University of Michigan Press, 1972), 417–18; Girilal Jain, *The Hindu Phenomenon* (New Delhi: UBSPD, 1994), 56–57.

3. A.L. Basham, *The Wonder That Was India*, 3rd ed. (London: Sidgwick & Jackson, 1967), 77–78.

4. Percival Spear, *op. cit.*, 465.

5. Ibid, 465.

6. For a more recent restatement, see Girilal Jain, *op. cit.*

7. Rudolph Peters, "*Jihād*," in Mircea Eliade, editor-in-chief, *The Encyclopedia of Religion* (New York: The Macmillan Company, 1987) Vol. 8, 88–89.

8. Seyyed Hossein Nasr, "Islam," in Arvind Sharma, ed., *Our Religions* (Harper San Francisco, 1993), 475.

9. *The Globe & Mail*, August 22, 1993, A7, emphasis added.

10. William H. Honan, "Into the Sheltering Arms of Evangelical Colleges," *New York Times*, Aug. 26, 1998, A20.

Discovering Zen

1. Daisetz Teitaro Suzuki, *Essays in Zen Buddhism* (New York: Grove Press, Inc. 1949), 188–89. It was all a funny story to me at the time, although the possibility that there might be more to it than the humor did dawn on me. It turned out that this interview itself has been virtually turned into a koan, as the following extract testifies:

BODHIDHARMA'S "VASTNESS!" From the Hekiganroku

> THE INTRODUCTION: To see smoke beyond the mountain is to know there is fire; to see a horn over the wall is to know there is an ox. From one corner displayed to know clearly the other three is only skill in inference, and to a monk an everyday affair. But when he can cut off all the streams of thought, he is free to spring up in the East or sink down in the West, to go against or with, along or across, to give or take. At that time say, of whom is this the action? Let us look at Setcho's riddle.
>
> THE CASE: The Ryo Emperor Bu asked the teacher Bodhidharma: "What is the first principle of the holy truth?"
>
> Bodhidharma said: "Vastness, no holiness!"
>
> Quoth the emperor: "Who is it that confronts Us?"
>
> Bodidharma said: "Know not."
>
> The Emperor did not understand, and Bodidharma crossed the river and went to Gi. Later the emperor asked Abbot Shiko, who said:
>
> "Does Your Majesty yet know who is this man, or not?"
>
> The emperor said: "(I) know not."
>
> Shiko said: "It is the Bodhisattva Kannon, who is transmitting the seal of the Buddha heart."
>
> The emperor in regret would have sent an envoy to ask him to return, but Shiko said:

"Though an emperor sends for an envoy for him, nay, though the whole people go after him, never never will he turn back."

THE HYMN:

The holy truth is vastness
How to speak and hit the mark?
"Who is it that confronts Us?"
and he replied.—"Know not."
So in the night he crossed the river.

How could he prevent the thorn-bushes growing after him? Though all the people pursue, he will not come again;

For a thousand, ten thousand ages we are thinking after him. Cease from thinking. The pure breeze,
circling the earth, has no bounds.

Setcho looks to the left and right, and says: "Is the Patriarch here?" He replies: "He is." "Then call him, that he may wash my feet."

VASTNESS, NO HOLINESS! From the Shoyoroku

THE INTRODUCTION: In olden days Benka offered an unpolished jewel to kings, but they thought it a pebble and punished him cruelly. At night a rare gem is thrown to a man, but in alarm he clutches for his sword. An unexpected guest, but none to play the host; the borrowed virtue is not the real virtue. A priceless treasure, but he knows not what to do with it; the head of a dead cat—try him with that!

THE CASE: The Ryo emperor asked the great teacher: "What is the first principle of the holy truth?"

Bodhidharma said: "Vastness, no holiness!"

Quoth the emperor: "Who is it that confronts Us?" Bodidharma said: "Know not."

When the emperor did not understand, the teacher crossed the river and went to Shorinji temple: nine years facing the wall.

nine years facing the wall.

THE HYMN:

Vastness, no holiness!

The moment came, but there was a gap between.

Like a master axeman, he would have cut the mud from the Face but never harmed the flesh—Oh profit!

Instead—Oh loss! The pot smashed to the ground, but he never turned his head.

Alone, alone, he sits at Sorinji in the cold;

Silent, silent, he upholds the great tradition.

In the clear autumn sky the moon's frosty disc is wheeling;

The Milky Way pales, the stars of the Dipper hang low.

When the heir comes, he in turn will receive Robe and Bowl;
From this arises medicine but also illness for men and gods.

(Trevor Leggett, *A First Zen Reader* [Rutland, Vt.: Charles E. Tuttle Company, 1960] 209, 211–12).

2. Takashi James Kudera, *Dogen's Formative Years in China* (Boulder: Prajñā Press, 1980), 60.

3. Ibid, 60–61.

4. Huston Smith, *The World's Religions* (Harper San Francisco: 1991), 133–34.

5. Joe and Guinevere Miller, *The Spiritual Teaching of Ramana Maharshi* (Boston & London: Shambhala, 1988), 74–75.

6. Apa B. Pant, "Awareness is All," in B.K. Ahluwalia and Shashi Ahluwalia, eds., *Maharshi Ramana: His Relevance Today* (Delhi: Vivek Publishing Company, 1980), 108.

Religions of India and China

1. G. Bühler, trans., *The Laws of Manu* (Delhi: Motilal Banarsidass, 1967), 33.

2. Quoted in Jawaharlal Nehru, *The Discovery of India* (New York: The John Day Company, 1946), 190–91.

3. Ibid, 190.

4. Cited in R.C. Majumdar, ed., *The Classical Age* (Bombay: Bharatiya Vidya Bhavan, 1970), 614.

5. Hartmut Scharfe, *The State in Indian Tradition* (Leiden: New York, 1989), 236.

6. Hemchandra Raychaudhuri, *Political History of Ancient India* (Delhi: Oxford University Press, 1996), 457.

7. Jawaharlal Nehru, *The Discovery of India* (New York: The John Day Company, 1946), 191.

8. K. Satchidananda Murty, *Revelation and Reason in Advaita Vedānta,* (Delhi: Motilal Banarsidass, 1974), 285.

9. Huston Smith, *The Religions of Man* (New York: Harper & Row, 1965), 35. Some have suggested that Jung took his cue from the yogas of Hinduism.

10. Cited in R.C. Zaehner, ed., *The Concise Encyclopedia of Living Faiths,* (Boston: Beacon Press, 1959), 260.

11. Alladi Mahadeva Sastry, trans., *The Bhagavad Gita with the Commentary of Sri Sankaracharya* (Madras: Samata Books, 1979), 2. See also Julius Lipner, *Hindus: Their Religious Beliefs and Practices* (London and New York: Routledge, 1994), 218.

12. Wm. Theodore De Bary, ed., *Sources of Chinese Tradition* (New York and London: Columbia University Press, 1960) Vol. I, 50; emphasis added.

13. Louis Renou, *Religions of Ancient India* (London: The Athlone Press, 1953), 54.

14. Huston Smith, *The World's Religions*, 215–16.

15. Kirin Narayan, *Storytellers, Saints and Scoundrels: Folk Narrative in Hindu Religious Teaching* (Philadelphia: University of Pennsylvania Press, 1989), 22–25.

Rediscovering Mahatma Gandhi

1. R.C. Rajumdar, ed., *Struggle for Freedom* (Bombay: Bharatiya Vidya Bhavan, 1969), 471–72.

2. Will Durant, *Our Oriental Heritage* (New York: Simon & Schuster, 1954), 389–633.

3. Cited in S.D. Kulkarni, ed., *The Study of Indian History and Culture* (Bombay: Shri Bhagavan Vedvyasa Itihasa Samshodhan Mandir, 1995), 22.

Montreal and After

1. R.N. Dandekar, *Exercises in Indology* (Delhi: Ajanta Publications [India], 1981), 9.

2. Harmut Scharfe, *The State in Indian Tradition* (Leiden: E.J. Brill, 1989), 69.

3. Ibid

4. Ibid, 67.

5. Hemchandra Raychaudhuri, *Political History in Ancient India* (New Delhi: Oxford University Press, 1996), 492.

6. J.A. Dubois, *Hindu Manners, Customs and* Ceremonies, ed. H.K. Beauchamp (Oxford: Claredon University Press, 1959), 11–12.

7. See Arvind Sharma, *Modern Hindu Thought: The Essential Texts* (New Delhi: Oxford University Press, 2002), 42.

8. This section is an enlarged version of my contribution to John Kelsay and Sumner B. Twiss, eds., *Religion and Human Rights* (New York: The Project on Religion and Human Rights, 1994), 68–70.

World's Religions After September 11

1. Tore Lindholm, W. Cole Durham, Jr., and Bahia G. Tahzib-Lie, eds., *Facilitating Freedom of Religion or Belief: A Deskbook* (Leiden: Martinus Nijhoff Publishers, 2004), xxix–xxx.

2. Arvind Sharma, "Terrorism and World Crisis: Finding Moral Compass on Ground Zero," *ARC: The Journal of the Faculty of Religious Studies at McGill University* (2002), Vol. 30: 237–38.

3. As cited in T. Patrick Burke, *The Major Religions: An Introduction with Texts* (Malden, MA: Blackwell Publishing Ltd., 2004), 312.

4. As cited in Mary Pat Fisher, *Living Religions*, 5th ed. (Upper Saddle River, N.J.: Prentice Hall, 2002), 366.

5. Paul Reps, *Zen Flesh, Zen Bones* (New York, Doubleday and Company, Inc., 1957), 35–36.

6. William Thorsell, "Whose Justice Is It?" *The Globe and Mail* [Toronto], January 9, 1999, D6.

7. Ramit Plushnick-Masti, "War Reparations with a Personal Touch," *The Gazette* [Montreal], January 2, 2005, IN5.

8. Alan Dershowitz, *Rights from Wrongs: A Secular Theory of the Origins of Rights* (New York: Basic Books, 2004), 124.

9. Based on Betty Debnam, "Rosa Parks, A Modern Heroine," *The Gazette* [Montreal], January 24, 2005, B8.

10. Tore Lindholm, W. Cole Durham, Jr. And Bahia G. Tahzib-Lie, eds., *op. cit.*, xix.

11. For answers to these questions see Arvind Sharma, ed., *Part of the Problem, Part of the Solution: Religion Today and Tomorrow* (Westport, Connecticut: Praeger, 2008), 101–103.

12. Cyril Northcote Parkinson, *Parkinson's Law: The Pursuit of Progress* (London: John Murray, 1958), passim.

13. Katherine Wilton, "Dawson Killer Eyed Four Schools," *The Gazette* [Montreal], January 18, 2007, 1.

14. Tore Lindholm, W. Cole Durham, Jr., Bahia G. Tahzib-Lie, eds., op cit, xxx.

15. Those who wish to see the statement unpacked may consult Phil Cousineau, *The Way Things Are: Conversations with Huston Smith on the Spiritual Life* (Berkeley: University of California Press, 2003), 23ff.

Conclusion

1. T.M.P. Mahadevan, *Outlines of Hinduism* (Bombay: Chetana Limited, 1971), 146.

2. M. Hiriyanna, *The Essentials of Indian Philosophy* (London: George Allen & Unwin Ltd., 1949), 163.

3. Resulting in Arvind Sharma, *Hinduism and Human Rights: A Conceptual Approach* (New Delhi: Oxford University Press, 2003).

4. Resulting in Arvind Sharma, *Are Human Rights Western? A Contribution to the Dialogue of Civilization* (New Delhi: Oxford University Press, 2006).